I'M A SPAM® FAN

FAN

America's Best-Loved Foods

CAROLYN WYMAN

LONGMEADOW PRESS

DEDICATION

To my brothers, Doug and Vern,
with whom I shared my first package of Yodels

Cover design by Mike Stromberg
Interior design by Philip Denlinger

Library of Congress Cataloging-in-Publication Data

Wyman, Carolyn.
    I'm a Spam fan: the stories behind America's favorite foods / Carolyn Wyman.
    p.   cm.
    1. Convenience foods—United States—Composition.
    2. Brand name products—United States—Composition.
    I. Title.
TX370.W95   1993
641.3¢1—dc 20   92-25148
                                                       CIP

ISBN 0-681-41445-6

Printed in Singapore
First Edition
0 9 8 7 6 5 4 3 2

Cheerios, Wheaties, Hamburger Helper, Tuna Helper, Betty Crocker, Gold Medal, Bisquick and Count Chocula are registered trademarks of General Mills, Inc.

Quaker, Rice-A-Roni, Aunt Jemima and Gatorade are registered trademarks of The Quaker Oats Company.

Nabisco, Triscuits, Grey Poupon, Fig Newtons, Oreos, Vermont Maid, Chips Ahoy!, Ritz and Barnum's Animals are registered trademarks of Nabisco Brands, Inc.

Planters, Mr. Peanut and Life Savers are registered trademarks of Planters LifeSavers Company.

Grape-Nuts, Kraft, Postum, Post, Entenmann's, Maxwell House, Baker's, Cappio, Sanka, Brim, Birds Eye, Jell-O, Cool Whip, Lender's, Philadelphia Brand, Philly, Velveeta, Handi-Snacks, Minute, Tang, Kool-Aid, Log Cabin and Cheez Whiz are registered trademarks of Kraft General Foods, Inc.

Budget Gourmet is a registered trademark of The All American Gourmet Company.

Chex is a registered trademark of Ralston Purina Company.

Wonder, Twinkies and Hostess are registered trademarks of ITT Continental Baking Company.

Kellogg's, Corn Flakes, The Sweetheart of the Corn design, Frosted Flakes, Tony the Tiger, Rice Krispies, Snap!, Crackle!, Pop!, Rice Krispies Treats, Fruity Marshmallow Krispies and Froot Loops are registered trademarks of The Kellogg Company and are used with permission.

Pepperidge Farm, American Collection and Orleans are registered trademarks of Pepperidge Farm, Inc.

Campbell's and Swanson are registered trademarks of The Campbell Soup Company.

Folgers is a registered trademark of The Folger Coffee Company.

Chun King is a registered trademark of Chun King International V. V.

Duncan Hines is a registered trademark of Hines-Park Foods, Inc.

Pringles and Crisco are registered trademarks of The Procter & Gamble Company.

Chock Full O' Nuts is a registered trademark of Chock Full O' Nuts Corporation.

Salada is a registered trademark of Redco Foods, Inc.

Celestial Seasonings and Red Zinger are registered trademarks of Celestial Seasonings, Inc.

Nestlé and Toll House are registered trademarks of Nestlé, Inc.

Stouffer's and Lean Cuisine are registered trademarks of The Stouffer Corporation.

Coffee-mate is a registered trademark of The Carnation Company.

Weight Watchers is a registered trademark of Weight Watchers International, Inc.

Star-Kist is a registered trademark of Star-Kist Foods, Inc.

Ore-Ida is a registered trademark of Ore-Ida Foods, Inc.

Healthy Choice is a registered trademark of ConAgra, Inc.

Minute Maid, Coca-Cola and Coke are registered trademarks of The Coca-Cola Company.

Häagen-Dazs is a registered trademark of Häagen-Dazs Licensing Corp.

Totino's, Bake-Off, Jeno's, Poppin' Fresh, Green Giant, Hungry Jack and Pillsbury's Best are registered trademarks of The Pillsbury Company.

Eskimo Pie is a registered trademark of Eskimo Pie Corporation.

Russell Stover is a registered trademark of Russell Stover Candies, Inc.

Reynolds is a registered trademark of Reynolds Metals Company.

Popsicle is registered trademark of Popsicle Industries, Inc.

Good Humor is a registered trademark of Good Humor Corp.

Heath is a registered trademark of L.S. Heath & Sons.

Ben & Jerry's, Chunky Monkey and Dastardly Mash are registered trademarks of Ben & Jerry's Homemade.

Sara Lee is a registered trademark of Sara Lee Corporation.

Lay's and Fritos are registered trademarks of Frito-Lay, Inc.

Jolly Time is a registered trademark of American Pop Corn Company.

Pam is a registered trademark of American Home Products Corporation.

Reddi-wip is a registered trademark of Beatrice Cheese, Inc.

Orville Redenbacher's and Hunt's are registered trademarks of Beatrice/Hunt-Wesson, Inc.

Cornnuts is a registered trademark of Cornnuts, Inc.

Slim Jim is a registered trademark of GoodMark Foods Inc.

B&M and Friend's are registered trademarks of Pet Incorporated.

Ragú is a registered trademark of Ragú Foods Co.

Cracker Jack, Borden, Eagle, Elmer's, Wise and Cheez Doodles are registered trademarks of Borden, Inc.

Spam is a registered trademark of Geo. A. Hormel & Company for luncheon meat.

Michelina's is a registered trademark of Luigino's, Inc.

Ocean Spray, Cranapple, Cran Grape and Cran Raspberry are registered trademarks of Ocean Spray Cranberries, Inc.

Uncle Ben's and Converted are registered trademarks of Uncle Ben's, Inc.

Lipton is a registered trademark of The Thomas J. Lipton Company.

Morton and "When it rains, it pours" are registered trademarks of Morton International, Inc.

Dr, Pepper, and Dr Pepper are registered trademarks of Dr Pepper Company.

Seven-Up and 7-Up are registered trademarks of The Seven-Up Company.

Hires is a registered trademark of Crush International, Inc.

Pepsi and Pepsi-Cola are registered trademarks of PepsiCo Inc.

Welch's is a registered trademark of Welch's Foods, Inc.

Hershey's, Hershey's Kisses, Chocolate World, Reese's, Reese's Milk Chocolate Peanut Butter Cups, Reese's Pieces and the conical configuration and plume device are registered trademarks of Hershey Foods Corporation and are used with permission.

Pop Rocks is a registered trademark licensed to Carbonated Candy Ventures.

Dove and M&M's are registered trademarks of Mars, Incorporated.

Sugar Daddy, Sugar Babies, Pom Poms and Junior Mints are registered trademarks of Warner-Lambert Company.

Wrigley's, Wrigley's Doublemint and Wrigley's Spearmint are registered trademarks of Wm. Wrigley Jr. Company.

Tabasco is a registered trademark of McIlhenny Company.

Hellmann's is a registered trademark of CPC International Inc.

Heinz is a registered trademark of H. J. Heinz Company.

Land O Lakes is a registered trademark of Land O' Lakes, Inc.

The Oscar Mayer Rhomboid and the Weinermobile are registered trademarks of Oscar Mayer Foods Corp.

Butterball is a registered trademark of Swift-Echrich, Inc.

Sun-Maid is a registered trademark of Sun-Maid Growers of California.

Chiquita is a registered trademark of Chiquita Brands, Inc.

Sunkist is a registered trademark of Sunkist Growers, Inc.

Dole is a registered trademark of Dole Food Company, Inc.

Keebler is a registered trademark of Keebler Company.

Sunshine and Hydrox are registered trademarks of Sunshine Biscuits, Inc.

In addition, the author gratefully acknowledges HarperCollins Publishers Inc. for permission to reprint an excerpt of "Animal Crackers" from Chimney Smoke by Christopher Morley, ©1917 by Harper & Brothers, and 1945 by Christopher Morley.

CONTENTS

ACKNOWLEDGMENTS

This book would just have been another one of my great ideas if it had not been for the help and forbearance of numerous friends, colleagues, librarians and food industry sources. Thanks first to my editors at the New Haven Register, past and present, for a work arrangement that has given me the time to do this and other projects. Thanks to Mary Jo Kochakian and Phil Greenvall for lending their professional expertise to a first reading of this manuscript and to Mara Lavitt, for taking the dust jacket photo. Thanks also to my agent, Madeleine Morel, and my editor at Longmeadow Press, Daniel Bial, for carefully spoonfeeding me my first taste of the book business.

For invaluable help in obtaining information and photographs used in this book I would also like to thank Kathryn Newton, E. Barry Wegener, Pam Becker and Jean Toll of General Mills; Ann Smith and Dave Stivers of Nabisco Brands; Niagara County historian Dorothy Rolling; Patrick Farrell for Ralston Purina; Cindy Harris, Myra Mack, Lisa Carlson and Laura Jackson of Quaker; Diane Dickey of Kellogg's; Ann Davin of Pepperidge Farm; Wendy Jacques and Ed Rider of Procter & Gamble; Angie Dorsey and Kathy Rouse for Celestial Seasonings; Joseph Breslin of Chock Full of Nuts; David Krutz of Redco Foods; Laura Watts of Coca-Cola Foods; Vickie Ayers and Robert Gould of Eskimo Pie; Lee Holden of Ben & Jerry's; Robyn Cohen of Cohn & Wolfe; Nancie Burger, Willie Evans and Jan Hough for Lender's; Rosalyn O'Hearn of Stouffer's; Susan Hanley of ConAgra; Marlene Johnson and Joe Andrews of Pillsbury; Susan Abitz of Gold Bond Ice Cream; Marsha Cade, Kevin Lowery, Judy Freedman, Megan McNichols and Joanne Marshall of Campbell's; Ann Haller of the Historical Society of Douglas County, Omaha, NE; and Bob Wheatley and Linda Massey for Sara Lee.

Also, Beverly Holmes of Frito-Lay; Kay Green of GoodMark Foods; Gina Chapman of the Snack Food Association; Heather Weigand, Ted Hake and Wes Johnson for Cracker Jack; Karen McRoberts and Julie Selsberg of Daniel J. Edelman, Inc.; Linda Mulrenan of American Home Foods; Kay Carpenter of Hunt-Wesson; John Gould, Ralph Cantisano and Deborah Jop for Ragú; Irene Sorensen, Betsy Parks and Cathy Loranger for Ocean Spray; Allan Krejci of Hormel; Dave Ahlgren, James Tills and Mark Maire for Chun King; Fran Sharp of Pet Incorporated; Marian Tripp and Claudia Hueser for Uncle Ben's; Anna Marie Coccia of Lipton; Erika Spoon of Rice-A-Roni; Kathleen Reidy of Morton Salt; Betsy Burstein, Nanci Edwards, Vanessa Simmons,

Mimi Minnick and Peter Liebhold of the Smithsonian Institution; Kathleen Esser of Creamer Dickson Basford; and Ellen Brown for Crisco.

Also, Marcia Fosnot of the Greenwich (CT) Library; James Weidman of Welch's; Philip Mooney of Coca-Cola; Andrew Whitman for Kool-Aid; Lynn Markley and Bob Stoddard for Pepsi-Cola; Judy Shirley of Pepsi-Cola 7-Up Bottling of Greenville, S.C.; Ann Taylor and Wynema Hamilton of Dr Pepper/7-Up; Robert Nedderman of Hasting College's Perkins Library; Bonnie Glass of Hershey Foods; Harriette Knox of Planters Life-Savers; Brenda Reed and Nancy Eckert of CC Ventures; Christina Oberman of M&M/Mars; Sandy Bell of Warner-Lambert; Linda Hanrath and Barbara Zibell of Wrigley's; Dick Curd of Carnation; Stephanie Bloom of Hunter MacKenzie Cooper; Beth Adams of Heinz; Elizabeth Strauss of Best Foods; St. Louis Post-Dispatch Library; Diane Rand of Kraft; Terry Nagle of Land O' Lakes; Alan Lowenfelds of Hotel Bar Foods; Gary Marshburn of Sun-Maid; Barbara Robison of Sunkist; Vickie Simms of Dole; Sharon Rahn and Jean Cowden of Oscar Mayer; Susanne Lam of Louis Rich; Stuart Greenblatt of Keebler; Cheri Carpenter, Huntley Baldwin and Rachel Boesing of Leo Burnett; and Kathy Oehme and Alex Nichols of Sunshine.

Also Jan Longone of the Wine and Food Library of Ann Arbor, MI; the staffs of the New Haven, Stratford, Fairfield and New Caanan (CT) public libraries; Amy Humphries of the Wallingford (CT) Public Library; Mitra Rastegar; and most especially, Becky Tousey of Kraft General Foods.

Many of these people also help Bonnie Tandy Leblang and me obtain information to write our syndicated newspaper column, Supermarket Sampler. I'd also like to thank Bonnie and the gang at Universal Press (especially Lisa Tarry, Lee Salem, John McMeel and Kathleen Andrews) for their belief in my ability to speak (and eat) for prepared foods fans everywhere.

Finally I'd like to thank Phil Blumenkrantz, whose patience while I worked on this book allows me to overlook his lack of judgment in preferring pudding to chocolate chip cookies.

INTRODUCTION

More Twinkies were sold this year than Madonna and Paul Simon's records combined. And yet much more is known about these personalities than America's favorite sponge-cake treat.

It's about time that injustice was corrected. For although ordinary, our all-American food products have their own stories that beg to be told. Did you know that Purina's checkerboard trademark was inspired by a poor family that founder William Danforth knew, who all wore clothes made from the same bolt of red-checkered cloth? That the medal on the Campbell's Soup label is a replica of an award the company's products won at the 1900 Paris Exposition? That the classic Coca-Cola bottle is shaped like a kola nut?

Like most members of the baby boom, I grew up eating food created by American technology: Reddi-wip and Velveeta, Hydrox and Hamburger Helper. I think I was 12 before I realized vegetables came in other forms besides cans and frozen blocks.

But it wasn't until I became a grown-up (?) and got a real job (?) as a writer with a column reviewing new supermarket food products that I realized it was impossible to talk about Smartfood without acknowledging its debt to Cheez Doodles. My appreciation led to a search to find out more about these pillars of the

check out lines—a search that led to the discovery that eating huge amounts of Shredded Wheat could make you high; that certain old Cracker Jack prizes are worth hundreds of dollars; that Twinkies were once used to capture baboons who escaped from an Ohio zoo. Was all this trivia really part of my American heritage, too?

Some may find my enthusiasm for these products out of step with new concerns about the contents of convenience foods and their effect on health. I never ask myself, "What the hell am I eating!" when I reach for another can of Jolt cola. I view current health concerns as just another craze. Back in the old days, most cereals and soft drinks were introduced as health foods. In fact, in 1916 Quaker Oats was advertised as a "vimfood which is 75% latent energy." Today it is being touted as "the right thing to do."

But people's concerns about the healthiness of these products are in most cases equally balanced with a certain fondness, or at least nostalgia. We sense this in David Letterman's jokes about the Keebler elves, in the Campbell's soup art of Andy Warhol, and in the Spam cooking contests held across the country.

Who can't remember having set up a Kool-Aid stand only to drink all the profits; having the fun of whacking a Pillsbury refrigerated dough can on the edge of a counter-top; or torturing their sensitive sister with the squeak of cardboard on cardboard as they ate a frozen push-up pop? Making Rice Krispies Treats for the very first time?

That's what this book is all about. So read on—about Ben & Jerry's very advanced degrees in the scientific methods of ice-cream making; why Hershey's chocolate drops are called Kisses; and who Doonesbury really is. Here's hoping the stories of America's favorite foods give you something to chew on long after you've finished eating.

Cheerios boxes through the years. Introduced as Cheerioats in 1942, the cereal became Cheerios in 1945. The 1949 box reflected the cereal's sponsorship of the Long Ranger TV show. Strawberries were added to the bowl of Cheerios, and a single Cheerio was used to dot the "i" in the box redesign of 1953. Used with permission of General Mills, Inc.

In the early days, the range of athletes who endorsed Wheaties was wider than it is today. Wild animal trainer Maria Rasputin appeared on this Wheaties package back in the 1930s. Used with permission of General Mills, Inc.

MARIA RASPUTIN

EUROPE'S SENSATIONAL WILD ANIMAL TRAINER
—FEARLESS DAUGHTER OF RUSSIA'S MAD MONK

"TO START THE DAY RIGHT, I ALWAYS RECOMMEND WHEATIES"

A "Breakfast of Champions"
PLENTY OF MILK OR CREAM AND SUGAR AND SOME KIND OF FRUIT AND

WHEATIES

Most commercial baked beans are produced using high–tech, rapid process, but following a long-standing New England tradition, B&M places theirs in pots and bakes them in brick ovens.

The motorized delivery truck, the bread-wrapping machine and the use of preservatives extended the shelf life for bread enough to allow Wonder to offer consumers this $1,000 freshness guarantee.

Chicago ad man Leo Burnett helped the Green Giant evolve from a scary, scowling creature in a bearwrap (left, 1927) to the jolly, smiling guardian of the growing fields consumers know today.

The Morton Salt girl has undergone five fashion make-overs since first appearing on the package in 1914.

Send C-Mail to the Wounded Over Here!

C-MAIL IS CHEER MAIL . . .
COOKIES, CAKES, CHOCOLATE

Uncle Sam's boys are well fed—no matter where they are.

But convalescent men, in hospital beds or wheel chairs, long for homemade sweets.

Send these homesick wounded a *real* taste of home. Cookies, for instance, that take them back to little-boyhood . . . that set them dreaming of sunny kitchens . . . Mom's Saturday bakings.

A *little* of your time will make a *lot* of happy time for them. Nothing will be so appreciated . . . nothing can so well show *your* appreciation of what they've done for you.

You know, of course, how soldiers go for Cookies. They love 'em! So be sure your C-Mail includes a generous quantity of various kinds.

A man doesn't have to be wounded to enjoy Toll House Cookies. But if he is, these golden, crunchy cookies made with Nestle's Semi-Sweet Chocolate are doubly precious, doubly good.

Chocolate is a fighting food. So if your dealer is temporarily short of Nestle's Semi-Sweet ask him to save you some when he gets it.

Send *C-Mail* Over Here
. . . *V-Mail* Over There

During World War II as in the Gulf War, Toll House Cookies were promoted as the perfect gift for troops at home and abroad.

Milton Hershey's business and philanthropic activities had such a profound impact on his hometown of Derry Church, Pennsylvania, that it was renamed Hershey in 1906. Today the streets of Hershey are illuminated by lights that look like Hershey's Kisses.

The creator of Welch's Grape Juice was a teetotaler and for many years the product was advertised as an alternative to wine. One of its most effective anti-alcohol campaigns featured a pretty woman insisting that "the lips that touch Welch's are all that touch mine."

Coca-Cola's tradition of holiday ads featuring Santa Claus, begun in 1931, is often credited with changing the way people pictured him. In the European tradition, St. Nicholas was a stern figure. But Coca-Cola officials instructed artist Haddon Sundblom to paint a Santa as big, warm, friendly and lovable as the Christmas holiday itself. Advertisement courtesy of the Coca—Cola Company.

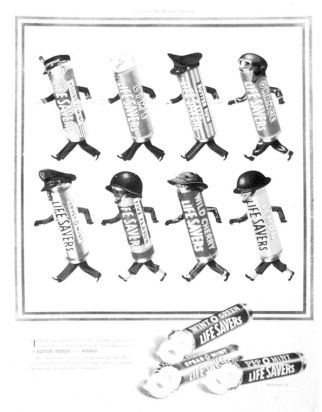

◀ Like M&M's, Life Savers were a popular mess kit candy during World War II because of their invulnerability to jungle heat. These parading military Life Savers were part of an ad to explain this as a reason for shortages of the candy back home.

False rumors that the little boy who played ▶ Mikey on the Life cereal commercials died from simultaneously eating Pop Rocks and drinking Coca-Cola failed to kill sales of the carbonated candy, which ricochets around the mouth in a most amusing way.

In the late 1800s, fruit growers identified their produce by packing them in wooden crates decorated with distinctive, colorful labels. Once the Southern California Fruit Exchange was formed, members of the cooperative wrapped their fruit in tissues emblazoned with the Sunkist name and often incorporated a picture of the tissue-wrapped fruit in their crate label designs.

Handpicking red peppers is a long tradition on Avery Island, home of Tabasco pepper sauce, as is the 3:30 PM weigh-ins and paying hour. Most of the island peppers are now harvested for seed used to grow the actual pepper sauce crops elsewhere.

A Sun-Maid packer named Lorraine Collett posed for this painting, later used as the raisin company's trademark, in 1915. It's interesting to note, given the product she represents, that the tray of grapes she posed with were artificial.

American consumers were just getting used to the idea of eating pineapple when, in 1934, two Dole engineers discovered a way to rupture the pineapple cells for juice. With Prohibition recently abolished, the exotic new drink was promoted as a great mixer with gin.

Ease and quickness of preparation continues to be a major selling point for Kraft Macaroni & Cheese, as it was in this 1940 ad. Kraft is a trademark of Kraft General Foods Inc. Reproduced with permission.

Oreo may be more popular but as this 1951 ad points out, Hydrox was America's first cream-filled sandwich cookie. Because Hydrox doesn't contain animal fats, it's long been the choice of vegetarians and those who keep kosher.

Finest ever made!

There is only ONE Sunshine HYDROX! HYDROX is the ORIGINAL...the masterpiece of all cream-filled chocolate cookies...the "Finest Ever Made."

Sunshine HYDROX COOKIES

THE ORIGINAL CREAM-FILLED CHOCOLATE COOKIE

CEREALS

CHEERIOS: NUMBER ONE WITH THE YOUNG

You might think that kids most popular cereal would be Count Chocula, Froot Loops or any one of the other fluorescent-hued, sugar-coated concoctions that appeal to hardly anyone over the age of reason. But according to most studies, it's Cheerios, that plain old oat cereal in the bright yellow box. It could be because Cheerios has stayed in step with kids for the past half century.

When Cheerios was first introduced in 1941, it was as sponsor of the popular Lone Ranger radio show. Before long, kids were pawing through the little dough-nut-shaped oat puffs for free silver-colored bullets or snipping models of frontier towns off the box back.

The Cheerios Kid began promoting Cheerios in the television ads of 1953. Thanks to the Cheerio bursting from his bicep, he emerged triumphant from every situation. (Photo used with the permission of General Mills, Inc.)

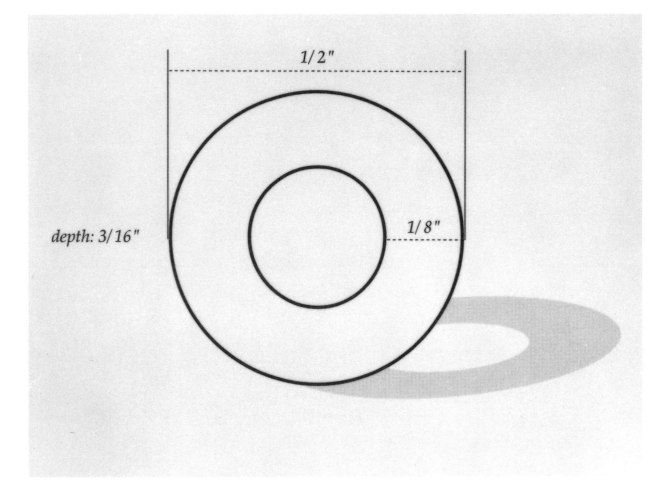

1/2"

depth: 3/16"

1/8"

General Mills researchers puffed up cooked grains in hundreds of shapes and sizes before coming up with the ½" × ⅛" × ³⁄₁₆" miniature oat doughnut that is Cheerios. (Photo used with the permission of General Mills, Inc.)

Parents like Cheerios because they're easy to digest and low in sugar. It's interesting to note that the sugar-enhanced Apple Cinnamon Cheerios was introduced the same year that regular Cheerios's advertising slogan became "lowest sugar of the leading brands." Honey Nut Cheerios, introduced in 1979, is now General Mills's second-best-selling cereal. Almost half of all American households are regular purchasers of one of the Cheerios three, or of Multi-Grain Cheerios, introduced in 1992.

How did such an American success story begin? Like many food products of the modern era, with scientific discovery, research and testing. In this case, the scientific discovery was a puffing gun developed by a Professor Alexander Pierce Anderson of Columbia University to make Quaker's Puffed Rice and Puffed Wheat cereals. General Mills's innovation was to use cooked oats instead of raw grains. Once fed into the machine's tubes, the oats burst into o's containing thousands of tiny air pockets, resulting in a cereal that not only looked like a tiny life preserver—it floated like one too.

Researchers experimented with many other shapes and sizes for the cereal, and conducted hundreds of consumer tests before coming up with the one-eighth-inch-wide circle with the hole and the name Cheerioats. The name was shortened to Cheerios in July, 1945, when Quaker Oats claimed they had exclusive right to have the word "oats" as a trademarked product name.

When 3-D was all the craze, General Mills included 3-D comic books inside. When everyone was tuning in to "American Bandstand," they featured phonograph records from that TV show as the premium. When Cheerios boxes contained imitation Confederate money in 1954, more such currency was distributed through the cereal than throughout the entire Civil War. In recent years, the big bowl of Cheerios on the front of the package has shared space with the Harlem Globetrotters, "Star Wars," Peanuts and the Muppets.

Cheerios even has a foothold among the under-two set. (The company estimates that 10 percent of all Cheerios are consumed by mouths as young as these.)

WHEATIES: BREAKFAST OF PRESIDENTS AND OTHER CELEBRITIES

Call it the power of suggestion. Call it superstition, for people under pressure to perform athletic feats are known to be superstitious. Whatever the reason, there are people who won't risk playing in a Little League baseball game or company outing volleyball tourney without first fortifying themselves with "the breakfast of champions"—those malty wheat flakes known as Wheaties.

Wheaties, long associated with specimens of physical strength and endurance, began with the theories of the owner of a Minneapolis fat farm. This particular health clinician (whose name has not been passed down to us) was cooking a batch of bran gruel for his patients one morning in 1921 when some droplets spattered on the hot stove, forming flakes. These were crisp and tastier than the food he was making. After making more in a griddle, he took his idea to executives at the nearby Washburn Crosby Company (the forerunner of General Mills). They liked the flakes but not the way they crumbled into dust when placed in a box. George Cormack, the company's long-time miller, decided to see if wheat flakes would hold up better. They did, and when flavored with a bit of malt syrup, sugar and salt, also tasted quite good. The product got its endearingly diminutive name from a company contest won by Jane Bausman, wife of the company's U.S. export market expert.

Wheaties was one of the first products to be advertised on radio. In fact, the success of a singing jingle in Minneapolis (and hope that similar ads could also boost sales elsewhere) is the only thing that kept executives from dropping Wheaties during a period of low sales in the late 1920s. Soon Wheaties was sponsoring whole radio shows, many aimed at kids. The best known of these shows featured Jack Armstrong, an adventurous all-American boy named after a childhood acquaintance of a General Mills executive. (The real Jack Armstrong was plagued by this connection as the radio character became popular and he began to receive hundreds of unsolicited phone calls. The real Jack also lost out on a job offer when a letter making him the offer was misdelivered to General Mills and buried in a pile of radio show fan mail.) As the series went on, Armstrong grew up into a young scientist so clever at anticipating the advances in the science of real weapons that during World War II, the U.S. government was compelled to screen and censor some scripts.

Wheaties was also one of the first cereals to offer premiums for box tops. One of the most successful offers, for a Jack Armstrong Hik-o-meter, literally cleared the grocery shelves of all traces of the cereal.

It wasn't until 1933—nine years after the cereal was first introduced—that Wheaties began its association with sports by sponsoring baseball radio broadcasts across the country. One of the first radio deals included use of a large signboard in the Minneapolis ballpark. When asked what the sign should read, Wheaties ad man Knox Reeves sketched a picture of the Wheaties package, thought a minute, then printed "Wheaties— Breakfast of Champions."

Early athlete endorsements of the product were made by Jack Dempsey, Johnny Weissmuller, Babe Ruth, and even wild animal trainer Maria Rasputin. In 1939, 46 of the 51 players selected for the Major League All-Star Game signed up to promote Wheaties. Other endorsements came unsolicited. When a competing cereal called Huskies began sponsoring the "Ripley's Believe It or Not" radio show, one of its most amazing episodes featured Lou Gehrig admitting that he ate Wheaties. In 1950 a 22-year-old Trenton, New Jersey man hoisted a 2,700-pound elephant on his back in front of 3,000 people, then declared, "There's only one thing I eat every day—Wheaties." (The man never received a red cent from General Mills.)

Although hundreds of athletes have endorsed the product on radio and television, the practice of featuring athletes on the cereal box didn't start until 1956. Since then, only seven have been chosen to appear on boxes of the cereal available all across the country. They are Olympic pole vaulting champion Bob Richards, Olympic decathlon champion Bruce Jenner, Olympic gold medalist and gymnast Mary Lou Retton, baseball's Pete Rose, football legend Walter Payton, tennis star Chris Evert and the current star, Chicago Bulls basketball player Michael Jordan. (In the 1980s, Wheaties also began featuring certain stars and cham-pionship teams on packages available in only certain areas of the country.)

The Bruce Jenner selection was attacked by an overzealous San Francisco assistant attorney general who said he didn't think Jenner ate Wheaties and cried consumer fraud. A San Francisco *Chronicle* cartoon of the time showed a SWAT team and the assistant D.A. shouting through a bullhorn, "We have you surrounded! Come out with your hands up, Wheaties!"

Of all the celebrities who have had a relationship with the cereal, one was an obscure Des Moines radio sportscaster who won Wheaties's most popular play-by-play announcer contest in 1937. The prize was an all-expense-paid trip to the Chicago Cubs spring training camp in Los Angeles. While he was there, Ronald Reagan was given a screen test at Warner Brothers studio. The rest of that story you undoubtedly know.

SHREDDED WHEAT: THE ORIGINAL NIAGARA FALLS CEREAL

Niagara Falls today is known as one of America's tackiest resorts: eastern headquarters for quickie marriages, motels with mirrored ceilings and a boat ride where everyone has to don rain slickers. In the early part of this century, however, it was also home to one of the wonders of the modern industrial age: the factory making Shredded Wheat. In fact, a pamphlet about Niagara Falls printed at the time intoned, "One might as well see Rome without seeing St. Peter's as to see Niagara Falls without visiting the home of Shredded Wheat."

Shredded Wheat was the invention of a middle-aged Denver lawyer named Henry Perky who had always been far more interested in get-rich-quick schemes than he had in drafting wills or pleading cases in court. Perky was almost 50 years old when, in 1890, he became interested in finding a way to process corn so that it could be dehydrated, yet remain edible. Perky asked an acquaintance who designed air brakes for a living, William Harry Ford, to help him make a machine that could process corn in this way. The machine consisted simply of a pair of rollers, one grooved and the other smooth, with a scraper attached. When a crank was turned, the rollers would press whatever came in between.

Ford once said he was the one who thought of feeding wheat through the machine. Another source says Perky got the idea from a man he met in a Nebraska

hotel restaurant who was eating boiled wheat. (The man told Perky that boiled wheat was one of the few foods that did not give him indigestion. Perky, who also had stomach problems, tried the food and agreed.)

Whatever the inspiration, Perky was soon feeding wheat through his machine and baking it to create a basketlike food we now know as Shredded Wheat. Instead of trying to sell the food, he first tried to sell the machine that made it. As an advertising sales tool, he opened a Denver restaurant where literally everything on the menu featured Shredded Wheat, including Shredded Wheat mashed potatoes, cakes, ice cream, and even coffee. He distributed recipes for banana croquettes with Shredded Wheat crumbs, creamed peas in Shredded Wheat baskets and fried mushrooms on split

Shredded Wheat biscuits.

When Perky finally realized that the market for Shredded Wheat was larger than the one for the shredding machines, he built the first of several manufacturing plants for his cereal. In 1895, he built a bigger manufacturing plant and invented Triscuit crackers, basically a thinner version of Shredded Wheat. The first Triscuits were about two inches wider than they are today and were put in packages with lightning rays, alluding to the fact they were baked in what where then most-amazing electric ovens.

By the start of the new century, Perky had begun making speeches hailing the health benefits of Shredded Wheat products. "From the most abject physical wreck, I have succeeded... in reorganizing my body

Visitors to the Shredded Wheat factory—and there were more than 100,000 per year—waited for tours to leave from a reception area that was decorated with leather-upholstered furniture, Oriental rugs and a crystal pendant that was illuminated by 36 electric lights.

into perfectly healthy condition. I use no other bread, nor cereal food product than Shredded Whole Wheat Biscuit and dishes made from these Biscuits. I am 55 years of age and feel younger than 20 years ago," he boasted. More modern research suggests a new reason why Perky may have felt great. Dr. David Conning, director of the British Nutritional Foundation, says a large bowl of Shredded Wheat could contain enough natural LSD—produced by a fungal infestation common to wheat—to induce mild euphoria in those not used to the drug.

Shortly after the power of Niagara Falls was first harnessed to produce electricity, Perky got a vision to build one of the most beautiful and modern factory buildings ever seen there and to invite visitors in as a way to advertise Shredded Wheat. In 1901, the first Shredded Wheat biscuit was made in the Niagara Falls plant, a five-and-a-half-acre building with air conditioning, a sparkling interior of white enamel and polished hardwood, and the hundreds of windows and 30,000 light bulbs that led it to be called "the Palace of Light." Employees also enjoyed marble bathrooms, an in-factory lending library, music and dance lessons, a company-sponsored band and choral society and such recreational facilities as a skating rink, a bowling alley and tennis courts. The factory was called "Perky's Palace," and compared to the dark and dirty factories most Americans were used to, it truly was a royal place. Situated within earshot of the falls, the palace was soon receiving 100,000 visitors a year, all of whom went home with a sample box of Shredded Wheat.

Perky retired shortly after the plant opened in Niagara Falls and died in 1906, at age 66. In 1928, his company was purchased by Nabisco, a company primarily known for making and marketing cookies and crackers. Recalled former Nabisco advertising manager Truman de Weese: "One chap wanted to dip [Shredded Wheat] in a chocolate bath...; others wanted to top it with some cheese or peanut butter." Nabisco ended up leaving Shredded Wheat alone. But based on consumer testing, the company did add some salt and vegetable oil to Triscuits.

Shredded Wheat and Triscuits are still made in Niagara Falls and boxes of the cereal still bear the words "The original Niagara Falls cereal" although it is now made by a different company (it became a Post cereal in early 1993) in a different factory that is not open to the public. Outdated as a manufacturing facility before World War II, the Palace of Light building became the home of Niagara County Community College (or, as it came to be known, Nabisco Tech) until 1973, then was sold to some developers who razed the building in 1976. It's now an empty lot. As Joni Mitchell sang, "They paved Paradise and they put up a parking lot."

GRAPE-NUTS: THERE'S A REASON THEY'RE SO WEIRD

Grape-Nuts is a mysterious food. It's made of neither grapes nor nuts and is as hard as tiny little rocks unless placed in a bowl with milk. Then it swells, like the Blob. So what the heck is it?

A bunch of very hard breadcrumbs made by combining whole wheat, malted barley flour, salt and yeast into a dough that's baked into loaves. Then the bread is shredded and baked again, this time very slowly, and ground up into the little nuggets we know as Grape-Nuts. Grape-Nuts's creator, C. W. Post, named it thus because he thought the repetitive baking had turned the bread starches into dextrose, or grape sugar, and because the cereal's hard nuggets reminded him of nuts.

Grape-Nuts was inspired by a granulated food Post had made to aid with his own digestive problems. After baking a wheat and barley mixture twice in his kitchen oven, he and his little daughter Marjorie would grind it up in a home grinder.

When Grape-Nuts was introduced commercially in 1898, it was the first widely sold cold cereal in America. It followed by only three years Post's successful introduction of Postum cereal beverage (see *Postum*), and the two proved to be perfect companion products. For one thing, the wheat husks that had to be stripped off to get the kernels for Grape-Nuts could be used as the bran for the Postum. The two products also each tended to sell best in opposite seasons: Postum in the winter and Grape-Nuts in the summer. But frugal New Englanders eventually latched on to a recipe that transforms the hardy Grape-Nut kernels into a tender and comforting winter pudding (see recipe below).

If you've ever wondered why the Grape-Nuts cereal box is smaller than most others, it's because Post said the cereal was concentrated. At the beginning, the package was brown and tan and contained a copy of Post's health tract "The Road to Wellville." Along with exercise, drinking lots of water and deep breathing, it recommended a balanced diet—and that meant Grape-Nuts for breakfast, Grape-Nuts for lunch and Grape-

Nuts sprinkled on salad for supper. Although Post's advertisements depicted "the Road to Wellville" as a yellow brick road-like trail to heaven, it was also what he called the long overhead conveyor that brought wheat from the grain tower to the bakery at his plant in Battle Creek, Michigan.

Other ads boasted of Grape-Nuts's powers in preventing appendicitis and helping to cure tuberculosis and malaria and make loose teeth tighter (although munching a few spoonfuls would seem more likely to make already-loose teeth fall out). The slogan "There's a Reason" appeared on most Grape-Nuts magazine ads (including one of a little girl that was painted by Norman Rockwell), although what for remained as mysterious to many people as the product's name.

Post created only one other cereal before his death in 1914. (He committed suicide during a bout of depression brought on by the failure of an experimental explosion to bring rain to a new city he had built in Texas.) It was a brand of corn flakes that debuted in 1904 under the name Elijah's Manna. But religious groups got so upset over his commercial exploitation of a Biblical character that he quickly renamed it Post Toasties.

Grape-Nuts Puff Pudding

1/4 cup butter or margarine
1/2 cup sugar or honey
1 teaspoon grated lemon rind
2 egg yolks
3 tablespoons lemon juice
2 tablespoons all-purpose flour
1/4 cup Post Grape-Nuts cereal
1 cup milk
2 egg whites, stiffly beaten

Beat butter with sugar and lemon rind until light and fluffy. Beat in egg yolks. Stir in lemon juice, flour, cereal and milk. (Mixture will look curdled.) Fold in beaten egg whites. Pour into greased 1-quart baking dish; place the dish in pan of hot water. Bake at 325 degrees 1 hour and 15 minutes or until top springs back when lightly touched. When done, pudding has a cakelike layer on top with custard below. Serve warm or cold with cream or prepared whipped topping, if desired. Makes 6 servings.

CHEX CEREALS: RALSTON PURINA PEOPLE CHOW

You might think people would balk at the idea of eating food created by a company best known for cow and dog food, but Ralston Purina has built a very successful business doing just that.

William Danforth was operating a feed business in St. Louis when he decided that the principles of healthy eating he used in making food for farm animals could be successfully applied to making breakfast food for people. To help increase acceptance for his first cereal, made of cracked wheat, Danforth had it endorsed by and named after Dr. Albert Webster Edgerly. Edgerly, better known as Dr. Ralston, was an advocate of healthy foods, including whole wheat cereal. In 1902, Danforth came up with a company name by linking Ralston's name with what he had originally planned to call the cereal—Purina (a word that had been inspired by an early company slogan, "Where Purity Is Paramount").

In time Danforth decided he needed a trademark to represent all Ralston Purina products and convey the wholesome values he believed they represented. In thinking about this problem, Danforth remembered a family in his hometown of Charleston, Missouri, that was so poor the entire family had worn clothes made from the same bolt of bright red-checkered cloth. Danforth thought that a red-and-white checkerboard trademark might make his products just as easy to spot. Soon after his products began bearing the checkerboard trademark, Danforth was wearing a red-check tie, jacket and socks to work. Eventually the address of the company became Checkerboard Square and Chex became the name for the company's most popular line of cereals, the delicate, basketlike cereal made of wheat (first appearing in 1937), rice (1950), corn (1958) and bran (1987).

Ralston Purina has in recent years also become the industry's leading producer of sugary cereals featuring such popular children's properties as G.I. Joe, Ghostbusters, Barbie and Donkey Kong—an accomplishment about which health food nut Danforth would probably be less than pleased.

In fact, by 1910 Danforth had superseded Dr. Ralston as a health advocate and inspirational speaker. A deeply religious man, he led his employees in prayer and calisthenics every day. From the checkerboard trademark, he developed a philosophy of the well-planned life, including social, mental, physical and religious activities. In 1932, Danforth gave over the reins of the company to his son, Donald, so he could devote more time to his interests in health and social activism through the nonprofit Danforth Foundation.

Donald sent the first known recipe for the company's

famous salty Party Mix snack to Ralston Purina's advertising agency in 1955, crediting it to his sister-in-law. Today consumers can buy Chex Party Mix Seasoning Packets (traditional or nacho flavored) or the mix itself, already made and boxed. (But you'll have to make it yourself if you want to include such popular variant ingredients as curry, coconut, peanut butter, popcorn or jelly beans.)

In addition to providing some ballast for cocktail drinking, Chex Mix has performed the more impressive function of helping to get William's grandson, John Danforth of Missouri, elected to the U.S. Senate. Thanks to the Ralston Purina fortune, he is still one of the richest men in the U.S. Congress.

Traditional Chex Party Mix

½ cup (1 stick) margarine or butter
1 ¼ teaspoons seasoned salt
4 ½ teaspoons Worcestershire sauce
8 cups of your favorite Chex brand cereals
1 cup salted mixed nuts

Preheat oven to 250 degrees. Melt margarine or butter in large shallow roasting pan in oven. Stir in seasoned salt and Worcestershire sauce. Gradually add cereal and nuts, mixing until all pieces are coated. Bake 1 hour, stirring every 15 minutes. Spread on absorbent paper to cool. Makes 9 cups.

Puffed Wheat and Rice: Shot from Guns

The Quaker Oats Company attracted thousands of people to its booth at the 1904 St. Louis World's Fair by setting up a battery of eight Spanish-American War cannons, loading them with rice, heating them in ovens, then wheeling them into a cage and firing. With a huge roar, hundreds of fluffy puffs of rice flew through the air, creating a miniature snowstorm. It was a demonstration of a new technique for cooking grain, but as far as Quaker officials were concerned, it had amounted to little more than a circus act, and an expensive one at that.

When Professor Alexander Pierce Anderson first told Quaker officials about this new exploding process of cooking he had developed, they had been excited enough to build him a secret laboratory where he could further his puffing experiments. Anderson had begun his exploration of cereal grains while working on his doctoral thesis. A botanist by training, he had been trying to figure out a way to break up starch granules so that they would be easier to digest. He stumbled on the answer when he read how scientists at the University of Munich expanded rice grains for easier study under the microscope by heating them up. Realizing the commercial implications of the process, he had patented it.

Because of the highly competitive nature of commercial cereal production, only the most senior members of Quaker management knew what Anderson was up to. While Anderson experimented on different grains, Quaker hired an engineer to design a puffing gun based on Anderson's patent that would produce enough puffed grain for a cereal factory. But by the time he had come up with something workable, several years later, Quaker officials had almost given up on the puffing project. It was only after Quaker Toasted Corn Flakes and Wheat Flakes were declared flops that they decided to try selling Puffed Rice and Wheat Berries (later changed to Puffed Wheat to make the two products easier to advertise in tandem). It was 1909.

Early ads for the product written by Claude Hopkins of the Lord & Thomas ad agency played on Americans' reverence for education by showing pictures of Professor Anderson and explaining how he had discovered the new process. Informed by the interest shown in the demonstration at the 1904 World's Fair, the ads also made much of the idea that the food was "shot from guns," as the product's slogan put it for many years. During that time, sales of the puffed cereals increased steadily.

But after Anderson's patent on the puffing process expired in 1929, the company had to do something extra special to distinguish itself from all the other puffed rice and wheat products that entered the market. In 1934, Quaker hired Babe Ruth to make personal appearances and do radio and Sunday comic ads for the cereals. Speaking directly to children, he said, "Live right, get plenty of sleep and eat right—if you want to make good in sports or in business. Eat lots of Puffed Wheat and Puffed Rice—they taste swell and they're good for you."

From 1935 to 1938, other celebrities were hired to endorse the cereal, including Shirley Temple, Fred MacMurray and Bing Crosby. Crosby said he liked to eat his Puffed Wheat with berries and cream cheese. MacMurray said he ate it with grilled mushrooms.

But for creativity, none of these could beat ad man Bruce Baker's idea to promote Puffed Rice and Wheat's sponsorship of a TV show about a mounted policeman of the Canadian Northwest called "Sergeant Preston of the Yukon" in 1955. The idea was this: Quaker would buy up a relatively inexpensive piece of land in Sergeant Preston's own Yukon

Territory then enclose deeds to square-inch parcels of it in the cereal boxes. One day after suggesting this, Baker, a Quaker representative and a lawyer were winging their way to the Canadian Northwest. When the three finally arrived in Dawson in their three-piece suits, they set off a rumor of a new gold rush that lingered the rest of the winter. Why else would people dressed like that be in town?

The trio met with a real estate agent and another lawyer and bought a 19-acre plot on the Yukon River for $10,000. The trouble started when the Quaker lawyer insisted on seeing it. Although parts of the river were already frozen, they were able to find a Canadian Mountie familiar with the TV show who was willing to bring them. Then, just as they reached the land they had bought, the Mountie's little outboard struck a submerged rock and nearly swamped. Luckily Dawson was downstream, so they were able to drift back to town after the nearly frostbitten visitors had had a brief look around. But when they were driving from Dawson to the airport and the car died, the three thought they would freeze to death for sure. Miraculously, a gasoline truck appeared—one of the few vehicles scheduled to travel that road all week.

The group returned and the scheme went forward. All 21 million deeds were given away, each one with its own letter and number to differentiate it from its neighbors. Then the real nightmares began: phone calls to see if the deeds had any actual value; calls from people who had collected thousands of one-inch square deeds and wanted to see if they could turn them into one big piece. A Quaker spokesman said the company still gets an occasional letter about the deeds. They may have sentimental or collectible value, but no legal value today.

Quaker won't go so far as to say they regretted the Yukon adventure, but later promotions for the Puffed cereals were more mundane—the offer of a bathroom scale (emphasizing the diet characteristics of the cereals) for $4.95 and a tiny snap cannon that came free in boxes in 1964, which merely drove mothers crazy with the noise.

KELLOGG'S CORN FLAKES: ITS INVENTOR HAD HIS FLAKY MOMENTS

Mom and apple pie are about the only things more mainstream American than Kellogg's Corn Flakes. But this product had its beginnings among some rather fanatical religious and health food organizations.

Corn flakes were invented in a Battle Creek, Michigan, area sanitarium owned by Sister Ellen Harmon White, a Seventh-Day Adventist leader who once sat in a laundry basket on a hilltop in Maine with other devoted Adventists waiting for God to take her to heaven. When He didn't, she decided to move to Battle Creek, and open a haven for those who wanted to remain pure in body and spirit. The Western Health Forum Institute opened its doors in 1866. But it wasn't until she hired Dr. John Harvey Kellogg, the author of several diet books, as director in 1876 that the newly renamed Battle Creek Sanitarium became a favorite retreat of such rich or famous people as John D. Rockefeller, Henry Ford, Theodore Roosevelt and, in her waning days, Sojourner Truth.

This was in spite of Kellogg's belief in complete sexual abstinence (he reportedly wrote "Plain Facts for Old and Young," an antisex tract, on his honeymoon) and some of the strange treatments he prescribed for various ailments. Skinny people were forced to eat 26 times a day and remain motionless in bed with sandbags on their stomachs (to facilitate food absorption). Those suffering from high blood pressure were put on a daily diet of 10 to 14 pounds of grapes—and nothing but grapes. At mealtimes other patients were encouraged to sing a song Kellogg had composed about the benefits of thorough mastication. Chewing dry, brittle food was particularly good for the teeth, Kellogg thought, but when one patient broke her false teeth on some zwieback the sanitarium was serving and asked for $10 to replace them, Kellogg set to work on creating a slightly less formidable food.

Having once met with Henry Perky, the inventor of Shredded Wheat, Kellogg knew that whole wheat could keep longer after it was shredded and cooked. Kellogg was in the midst of an experiment with some boiled wheat one day when he was called away by a medical emergency. When he ran the wheat through a roller the next day, he expected it to come out in one huge sheet. But instead there were individual flakes that, when baked, were tastier than the other foods his guests were used to being served. By letting the dough stand, moisture had gotten into each individual wheat berry in a process cereal makers now call tempering.

Soon Kellogg had a thriving mail-order business selling wheat and corn versions of his new flaked food. Kellogg refused to taint the medical reputation of his clinic by selling his food in stores. But Kellogg's brother, Will, had no such reservations. John Kellogg had hired Will as his right-hand man or, as Will thought of it in darker moments, his flunky. Sanitarium staff got used to seeing J. H. riding his bicycle around the grounds with Will trotting alongside, taking notes on his brother's plans.

A lot of people were surprised when, in 1906, the 46-year-old Will had the gumption to buy the commercial rights to the corn-flaked cereal from his brother and the smarts to turn it into a best-selling brand. First he added malt, sugar and salt to improve its taste—

changes that prompted the first of a series of lawsuits from his appalled doctor brother. Will then wrapped the box in wax paper to keep the flakes fresh (later figuring out how to put the wax paper inside the box, thus saving two inches of paper per wrapping or $250,000 a year). He took the "Sanitas" name off the box because, he said, it had "the connotation of plumbing, washable oilcloth, wallcovering and refrigerators." To distinguish his product from dozens of imitators, he put "The Genuine Bears This Signature—W. K. Kellogg" on every carton.

Will had equally good ideas about advertising. In one 1907 ad considered quite risqué, Will declared Wednesday "Wink Day" in New York and offered a free box of cornflakes to every woman who winked at her grocer on the appointed day. Another contrary campaign urged people to stop eating Kellogg's Corn Flakes so their neighbors would be able to find some. In 1911, he erected a block-long electric sign in New York City's Times Square that featured a boy crying electric tears until the words "I got Kellogg's Toasted Corn Flakes" appeared.

Will didn't get along too well with his heirs and so gave most of his fortune to the Kellogg Foundation to help needy children. Both Will and John Kellogg died at age 91, still on the outs with each another. John wrote one reconciliatory letter to Will, but by the time Will received it, John was already dead.

The Kellogg Company discontinued its famous plant tour in 1986, citing concern with industrial espionage (mainly from European firms) and product safety (this was the time of the Tylenol scare). Still the Battle Creek Adventist Hospital in Battle Creek administers a small museum in Kellogg's first factory building, and tours of the original sanitarium building, across the street at 165 N. Washington St., are given by appointment (tel.# 616-964-7121). Kellogg's headquarters also has a display of historic photos and memorabilia, and if you peer through a fence at 235 Porter St. by the Kellogg factory, you can see statues of Kellogg's Frosted Flakes spokescats Tony the Tiger and Tony Jr.

BREAKFAST WITH SNAP! CRACKLE! AND POP!

If you ever find yourself on stage trying to entertain a hostile audience, try singing the jingle, "Snap! Crackle! Pop! Rice Krispies."

That's the strategy employed by one American nightclub act, who says the song never fails to draw applause: a testimony to the enduring popularity of the cereal, the song, and for the three elves who sang it.

Although Rice Krispies® advertising copy was quick to point out the way the cereal made noise in milk, the Snap!® Crackle!® and Pop!® cartoon trio didn't appear until almost a decade after the cereal's 1928 introduction. In 1933, a tiny gnome wearing a baker's hat appeared on a Rice Krispies side panel. His two sidekicks joined him in print ads within a year or two but not on the boxes and movie shorts until the late 1930s. During World War II, the trio posed patriotically with guns, tanks and ships in ads that urged consumers, "Save time, save fuel, save energy."

The early versions of Snap!, Crackle! and Pop!, created by children's book illustrator Vernon Grant, had huge ears and noses and slits for eyes. A major design overhaul in 1949 brought their features down to more human proportions, with minor tweaking employed since. The hats are the one constant: Snap! always wears a baker's; Crackle!, a red-and-white-striped stocking cap; and Pop!, an old British-style military one.

The main reason the characters exist at all, of course, is because the cereal makes noises when milk is poured on. Or, as the 1932 ads put it, "So crisp, it crackles in cream." The company says the sound is caused by the tiny air bubbles each toasted puff of rice

"I'm not missing a word"

A close listener picks up quite an earful around Kellogg's Rice Krispies. You pour on milk or cream and they tell you in no uncertain terms how crisp and fresh they are. But their famous "Snap! Crackle! Pop!" is all the world's only talking cereal ever says. If you want the story on all its vitamins, minerals and energy generators, better pick up a spoon and get next to a bowl. How about tomorrow?

By 1955 Snap! Crackle! and Pop! had more human features—and competition from a cute little boy in this *Life* magazine ad.

contains. When milk is added, it is unevenly absorbed by the puffs, causing the puffs to strain and stretch.

The famous sound is what happens when some of the starch in the cereal breaks down under that strain. (Of course, this does not explain why Rice Krispies bought in Sweden instead make noises like "Piff! Paff! Puff!" and in South Africa, "Knap! Knaetter! Knak!")

Sometime in the late 1930s or early 1940s, Kellogg Kitchens™ came up with a recipe to mix Rice Krispies with marshmallows that quickly became an afterschool favorite. Not only does it take a few minutes to make, it doesn't require cooking and the Krispie cakes can be molded into all sorts of fun shapes. The popularity of these treats even inspired two new kinds of Kellogg's Rice Krispie cereal: Fruity Marshmallow Krispies® and Rice Krispies® Treats Cereal.

QUAKER OATS: THE FRIENDLY CEREAL

In 1989, Popeye made a significant change in his diet. In place of spinach, he began eating Quaker Instant Oatmeal. After beating up archenemy Bluto or punching out a shark in ads for the cereal product, Popeye declared, "I'm Popeye the Quaker man."

But Popeye didn't know what trouble was until those ads were viewed by the real Quakers, a religious group that holds nonviolence to be a central tenet of their faith.

"This is completely obnoxious and offensive," said Elizabeth Foley, spokeswoman for the Philadelphia Yearly Meeting, the largest Quaker group in the East. "We are an organization of pacifists.... To portray us as a church that beats up on other people is not okay."

It was not the first time that the Quaker people, or,

as they are also known, the Society of Friends, had objected to the Quaker Oats Company's use of their name. In 1915, the Friends went so far as to petition Congress to make it illegal to use the name of a religious group on a commercial product. Outlobbied nationally, the Quakers tried a similar action in state legislatures but succeeded only in Indiana.

Quaker Oats was formed in 1891 when seven independent millers, none Quaker, joined together to form what critics called "the oatmeal trust." The president of one of these predecessor companies, Henry D. Seymour, had chosen the name Quaker because he wanted his company's products to be viewed as wholesome, honest and pure as members of the religious group he had read about in an encyclopedia. His partner, William Heston, had a company trademark drawn of a William Penn look-alike holding a scroll that read "pure."

At the time, oatmeal was sold in grocery stores in open barrels, where it had a tendency to go bad or become rodent infested, so oatmeal millers thought an oatmeal advertised as "pure" would be particularly salable. To ensure this purity, the new oatmeal conglomerate packed its oatmeal in individual consumer-size containers and promoted it like nobody had ever promoted anything before. In 1891, the company hired five portly men to dress like Quakers and sat them on top of the engine and cars of a train running from Cedar Rapids, Iowa to Portland, Oregon. At every stop, they would jump down and distribute free sample boxes of Quaker Oats (the first example of trial-size sampling in history). Quaker president Henry Parson Crowell also directed one of the first efforts to put premiums inside product boxes—some early boxes of Quaker included silverware, china saucers, glass bowls or drinking glasses in addition to the cereal.

Crowell had ads for Quaker Oats painted on billboards, covered bridges, barns and even Britain's White Cliffs of Dover (the latter caused so much controversy that it was eventually removed by an act of Parliament). In newspapers and farm reports he placed advertisements that called Quaker Oatmeal "a dainty" and a "vim-food which is 75 percent latent energy." Another ad pointed out, "In the homes of the educated, the prosperous, the competent, seven out of eight regularly serve oatmeal." but that "hardly two percent of prisoners in four great penitentiaries were fed on oatmeal in their youth." By 1918, all Crowell's efforts had paid off in annual sales of $123 million, making Quaker Oats one of the largest companies in the nation.

Quaker Oats could have used a marketing genius like Crowell to deal with the 1989 Popeye flap and environmental groups' protests when Quaker changed the oatmeal container's lid from cardboard to plastic that same year. Given these recent problems and the advanced age of its typical consumer (grandfatherly spokesman Wilfred Brimley is their contemporary), one might wonder why the latest drawing of the Quaker Man is smiling so wide. Simply because Quaker still beats all the competition in hot cereal sales.

BREADS AND BAKED GOODS

PEPPERIDGE FARM: THE BREAD AND COOKIE CURE

One of America's largest producers of premium-quality breads and cookies grew out of a mother's search to find a cure for her son's asthma.

In 1935, one of Margaret Rudkin's three young boys was diagnosed with a serious asthmatic condition. For nearly two years, the Fairfield, Connecticut resident made the rounds of doctors and specialists, trying to see what could be done to help Mark. A doctor she particularly liked said that asthmatics are often allergic to ingredients added to processed foods and suggested she should restrict her son's diet to foods without these additives. Since no commercial breads met that criterion, Rudkin decided to make her first-ever loaf of scratch bread.

It "should have been sent to the Smithsonian Institute as a sample of bread from the Stone Age, for it was as hard as a rock and about one inch high," she later recalled. But subsequent efforts were better, and when she gave a sample of the stone-ground whole wheat loaf to her son's doctor, he ordered some for himself and recommended it to other patients.

Soon Rudkin had a nice little mail-order business running out of her kitchen, catering mainly to allergy doctors and their patients. On the suggestion of friends, she took samples of the bread to a local grocer. Although she was asking two and a half times the going price of 10 cents a loaf, it tasted so good he agreed to carry it. When Rudkin got home, the grocer was on the phone, saying he was already sold out and asking when he could get another order.

Rudkin got her first New York City account using the same method. Although the "Pepperidge Farm Remembers" ads feature a horse and buggy, her first New York orders were actually delivered by her husband, a Wall Street stockbroker who commuted into the city every

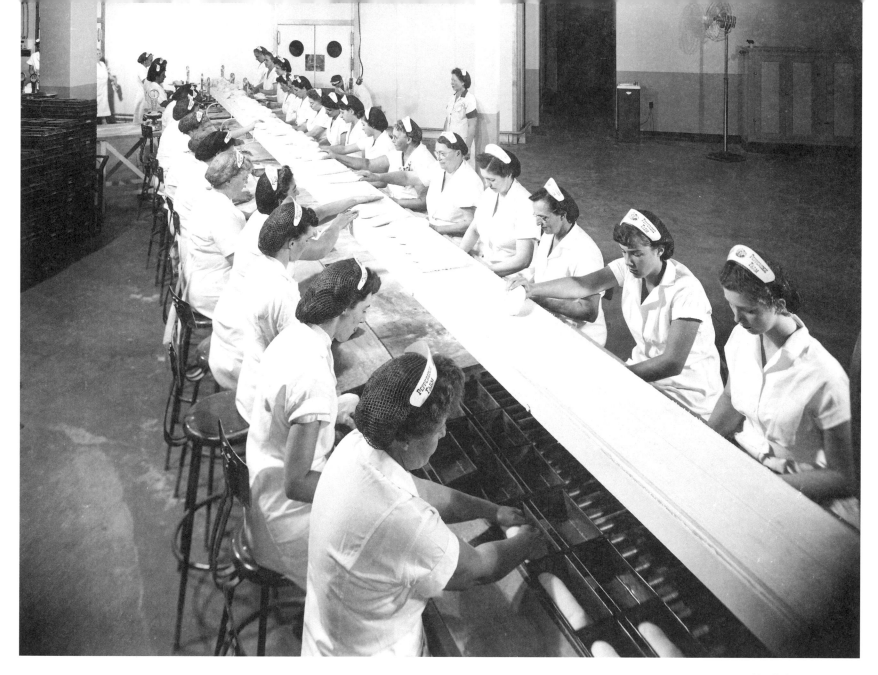

day by train. When he got to Grand Central Station, he handed a 25-pound package of bread to a porter who was paid 25 cents to run it to a store. Rudkin's first employees were all women who knew nothing about baking bread—that way, she could be sure things were done the way she wanted.

The Rudkins had purchased a 125-acre property

when they moved to Connecticut, calling it Pepperidge Farm after a species of sour gum trees that grew there. As her line of breads expanded to include white and raisin and sales grew, Rudkin moved operations from her kitchen to a garage, then to the horse stables— empty since her husband had been hurt in a riding accident. In 1947, the first real Pepperidge Farm bak-

Until the end of World War II and the opening of Pepperidge Farm's first modern bakery, company employees kneaded the bread dough by hand.

ery was built in nearby Norwalk, Connecticut.

In 1953, Rudkin introduced a line of Pepperidge Farm butter cookies, then withdrew them from the market within a year when they didn't live up to her standards. Not long afterward, on a trip to Europe with her husband, Rudkin found just the cookies she was looking for being made by the Delacre Company of Belgium. Pepperidge Farm entered into an agreement with the company and in 1955 began producing the fancy new cookies under the names of classy European locales. As with the breads, Pepperidge Farm cookies do not use inexpensive ingredients. When the price of the dark Belgium chocolate the company was using to drench its Orleans wafers became prohibitively exorbitant, the company simply stopped making them for a while. But a flood of mail from distressed consumers convinced them to bring them back with a hefty price increase.

More recently, the company has had great success with its American Collection. This is a line of large-size cookies so full of nuts and candy that the food technologists who developed them had trouble figuring out how to keep them together. Today cookies account for about half the company's business.

Pepperidge Farm became part of Campbell's in 1961, but Rudkin stayed on as chairman of the board of Pepperidge Farm until her death in 1967. Until his retirement in 1991, that title was held by Bill Rudkin, one of the three sons who tasted that first, museum-quality loaf of Pepperidge Farm bread.

THE WONDER OF BREADS

In these days of health fanaticism, saying you eat Wonder Bread is sort of like admitting to watching three or four hours of game shows and soap operas every day. In fact, the phrase "white bread" has become a fashionable put-down, meaning that someone or something is bland or uninteresting.

These people are too snobby and jaded to see Wonder as the simple showcase of flavors that it is. Peanut butter and jelly on rye or whole wheat, for instance, is simply a war of flavors, whereas peanut butter and jelly on Wonder are perfect harmony.

Commercial production of white bread began shortly after the invention of the bread-wrapping machine and the motorized delivery truck. Wrapping extends shelf life, and the trucks brought in the large egg, milk and flour orders needed to make the bread and speed delivery of the final product to retail outlets.

The Taggart Baking Company of Indianapolis (later Continental Baking) was the first to take advantage of the new technology when, in 1920, it came out with a one-and-a-half-pound loaf Taggart vice president Elmer Cline dubbed Wonder to call attention to its increased size. A decade later Wonder became the first bread to be available sliced, an innovation that boosted sales and gave rise to the expression, "the greatest thing since sliced bread."

The design scheme for the bread's wrapper came to Cline one day when he saw the sky near his house in Indianapolis fill up with colorful balloons that were competing in the International Balloon Race. To him, the balloons embodied wonder. That's how packages of the bread ended up featuring red, blue and yellow balls.

In 1941 Continental Baking Company joined in a government program to enrich white bread with some of the vitamins and minerals lost when whole wheat flour is bleached and milled into white. This program virtually eliminated such deficiency diseases as pellagra and beriberi from the land at a time when many people could not afford to buy many varieties of nutritious foods.

Although Wonder Bread never did "build strong bodies 12 ways" (the claim was ruled deceitful by the Federal Trade Commission in 1973 and disappeared from product advertising), it is better for you than many might think. When Consumers Union performed animal growth studies comparing various breads as an only food, the whites actually performed somewhat better than the wheats.

ENTENMANN'S: AMERICA'S SWEETS SUPPLIER

The chief bakers at Entenmann's don't have to worry about getting hungry: three times a day, every day, they meet for "scoring sessions" where they taste and rate products coming off Entenmann's factory line. Any product that doesn't rank at least 8 on a scale of 10 never leaves the building.

That's one method the company has used to maintain quality at America's largest bakery. Another is by processing most of its own ingredients. For instance, the company makes its own chocolate from cocoa powder imported from Holland (using about 75 thousand pounds of it a week) and cuts, chops and bakes its own apples at a plant dedicated to this purpose in the heart of New York's apple-growing country.

Entenmann's began as a home-delivery bakery service in 1898 in Brooklyn, New York. Owner William Entenmann drove the first horse and delivery wagon (a drawing of which is now the company logo). In the early 1900s, William's son contracted rheumatic fever, and on the advice of a doctor, the family moved to the then pastoral-like setting of Bay Shore, Long Island. There William opened a retail outlet as well as a bakery delivery service to homes and local delicatessens.

The business continued to grow under the leadership of William's son, William Jr., with little change in philosophy or goals. But when William Jr. died of a heart attack in 1951, his three sons and wife decided that the best way to reach the growing number of suburban customers on Long Island was to sell their products in supermarkets.

In this setup, still in place today, Entenmann's baked goods are sold through 850 truck drivers who earn up to $50,000 a year selling and displaying products in grocery stores and bringing out-of-date ones to company thrift shops. On their off hours, factory workers play in bowling league teams named the Brownie Rings, the Party Cupcakes, the Honey Loaves and the Raspberry Twists.

Entenmann's products became national after the company's sale to General Foods in 1982. The food scientists at General Foods helped Entenmann's to develop the first line of fresh cakes and pastries to contain no fat or cholesterol.

But the company's best-selling products are still their deliciously fat- and calorie-filled chocolate chip cookies, chocolate frosted doughnuts, golden pound loaf, raspberry danish twist and crumb coffee cake.

THE TWINKIE DEFENSE

It's impossible to talk about the corruption of innocents without thinking about the role Twinkies played in the trial of Dan White. White was the former San Francisco city supervisor who shot and killed Mayor George Moscone and Supervisor Harvey Milk in 1979. In attempting to defend White, attorney Douglas Schmidt argued that White's mental capacities had been impaired by his high intake of junk food—including Twinkies.

The jury apparently bought the argument, for White was acquitted on the murder charge and found guilty only of voluntary manslaughter. Schmidt's argument became known forever after as "the Twinkie defense."

Twinkies were also blamed for the theft of a bakery delivery truck in Marysville, Michigan, in 1975. Police found the truck minus the 1,800 Twinkies it had been carrying. In another Twinkie-related crime, a house in Kennett Square, Pennsylvania was burglarized twice in the same year. Each time the culprits overlooked the other valuables but took the Twinkies.

Fortunately most people can afford simply to buy their Twinkies. As a result, the creme-filled sponge-cake treats remain Continental Baking Company's best-selling item.

Twinkies were invented by James A. Dewar, a Hostess plant manager who saw the need for a new, low-priced product during the Depression. Aware that Continental sponge shortcake pans sat idle for all but the six weeks of the strawberry season, he got the idea of baking more cakes, injecting them with a banana filling (changed to vanilla when bananas got scarce during World War II) and selling them year-round.

The name was taken from a billboard advertising Twinkle Toe Shoes that Dewar and a friend saw during a business trip to St. Louis. In light of their oblong shape, the friend suggested he call the cakes "Twinkle Fingers." The name was later shortened simply to Twinkies.

Twinkies caught on quickly and it's no surprise. Like Wonder Bread (also a Hostess product) and Robert Redford, Twinkies are bland and vanilla, easy to digest and easy to mold and shape. (If you've ever had a grocery clerk put a quart of milk on top of your Twinkies, you know what I mean.) Although it has neither chocolate nor icing, the sugar-enhanced creme somehow manages to satisfy the sweetest sweet tooth. Among the cake's biggest fans are Howdy Doody (who touted them on his TV show in the '50s), Archie Bunker (who got one in his lunchbox every day), Jimmy Carter (who's rumored to have had a Twinkie vending machine installed at the White House) and a man who Continental Baking claims subsisted on nothing but Twinkies and Cutty Sark for several years.

Hostess executives say many people ask how the creme filling gets inside. The answer is that after the cakes are baked and cooled, the creme filling is forced in through three syringe-like air-fired injection tubes.

Twinkies have also been used to save the life of an elephant who refused to eat after surgery. The vet prescribed Twinkies, and the elephant got well. When baboons escaped from a zoo in Kings Mill, Ohio, in 1976, they were successfully recaptured only when someone got the bright idea of luring them into a cage with several unwrapped Twinkies.

Hostess thought long-time spokesperson Twinkie the Kid of "Howdy Doody" fame had ridden into the sunset until 13-year-old Judd Slivka of Livingston, N.J. started a petition drive that returned the cartoon cowpoke to Twinkies packaging in time for the snack cake's 60th anniversary in 1990.

COFFEE AND TEA

MAXWELL HOUSE: THE FIRST DROP WAS HARD WORK

In these days of gourmet specialty coffees and espresso machines, Maxwell House coffee might seem as ordinary as white bread. But in 1873, when Joel Cheek was selling grocery products on horseback in Tennessee, there were no decisions to make about brand or variety of beans. You just bought one brand of bean, unroasted, unground and packaged in a plain brown paper bag. Cheek had the idea that a blend of several different kinds of roasted coffee beans might taste better.

After experimenting on evenings and weekends, Cheek quit his job in 1882 to devote himself fulltime to the project. When he had the blend of flavors he wanted, he took it to the Maxwell House Hotel in Nashville. Hoping to gain from the association with that epitome of Southern hospitality, Cheek offered to let the hotel use it as the house blend. The coffee found such a good reception among the hotel's guests (which included Sarah Bernhardt, Buffalo Bill Cody, Enrico Caruso, Henry Ford, John Philip Sousa and at least seven U.S. presidents) that Cheek adopted its name for the coffee.

Although Cheek came up with the dripping coffee cup logo, Theodore Roosevelt is credited with the accompanying slogan. In 1907, while a guest at the Hermitage—Andrew Jackson's home in Nashville—Roosevelt was asked if he would like to have another cup of Maxwell House coffee. "Will I have another? Delighted!" he exclaimed. "It's good to the last drop." (Hal Morgan, in his book *Symbols of America,* suggests that Cheek could alternatively have picked up the expression from "last drop" campaigns then used by

Baker's Chocolate and Peninsular Paints.)

Although the expression is now so familiar it is hardly ever thought about, at the time it caused people to wonder, "What exactly is the matter with the last drop?" (One ad campaign answered by saying, "And that's good too.") Others questioned the use of the word *to,* a dispute that was resolved only when a professor of English at Columbia University checked the classics and concluded that this was indeed proper grammatical use.

In more recent years, controversy stirred over 1989 Maxwell House television ads that featured respected TV journalist Linda Ellerbee "reporting" on a national test that showed people preferring Maxwell House to Folgers. A *New York Times* op-ed piece complained that she was trading on her journalistic credentials in a misleading and unprofessional way. Ellerbee expressed some embarrassment but said she needed the money to start her own Lucky Ducky TV company. (And, as she would say, so it goes.)

Executives at General Foods, which purchased Maxwell House from Cheek in 1928, have also been challenged by declining coffee sales, particularly among young people. In 1962 about 75 percent of all Americans drank coffee; in 1989, only half of Americans did. In 1992, Maxwell House attempted to meet the new morning cola drinkers halfway by introducing Cappio, a cold cappucino drink.

MOUNTAIN GROWN, MRS. OLSON– RECOMMENDED FOLGERS

Forget Dr. Ruth, counseling or a long weekend away for just the two of you. What can really save a marriage is a can of Folgers Mountain Grown. That's what the Swedish-born Mrs. Olson told young wives whose husbands were unhappy with the coffee they made. For two decades, Americans drank up both the ads and the coffee.

Folgers's spokeswoman may have come from Europe, but the company was founded on principles as American as James Folger's dream of making lots of money in the gold rush. In 1849, James and his elder brothers Edward and Henry left their home in Nantucket, Massachusetts for San Francisco and what they hoped would be sure fortune. But when the brothers discovered they had only enough money for two of them to travel on to gold country, James agreed to be the one to stay behind.

James's first job was to help build a spice and coffee mill for William Bovee. Bovee had had some experience in the business of roasting and grinding coffee for the upper classes in New York City. With so many ships going through the Isthmus of Panama to bring hopefuls to the gold rush, Bovee thought it would be easy to get supplies of coffee grown on mountain slopes in Central America.

At that time, most ordinary people roasted their own coffee at home. But with the primitive conditions in the mining camps making that more difficult, he thought there might be many gold rushers who would be willing to buy roasted and ground coffee as well. He turned out to be right. As his company grew, Bovee gave Folger a job as clerk and salesman. Folger became a partner in the company in 1859. In 1865, he bought his partner out and renamed the business after himself.

Over the years, the company enjoyed many firsts: the first coffee company to have its own salesman, the first to sell a uniform roast and blend, and, since Procter & Gamble took over in 1963, the first national coffee brand to give Maxwell House some serious competition. From commanding 15 percent of all coffee sales in 1978, Folgers grew to a 27 percent share—or neck and neck with Maxwell House—in 1989.

That was also when Mrs. Olson's boast about Folgers being mountain grown ("It's the richest kind!") ceased to seem such an asset. In November of that year, Salvadoran government troops murdered six Jesuit priests.

American political activists believed the troops had been backed by Salvadoran coffee growers who were supported, in turn, by Folgers's large purchases of Salvadoran coffee. So the activists began a boycott of the coffee.

The boycott seems not to have hurt sales much, maybe because its effects were counteracted by a new series of ads featuring the slogan, "The best part of waking up is Folgers in your cup." Mrs. Olson was dumped in 1984, probably because in this day and age, a young woman faced with a husband who complained about her coffee would probably just tell him to make the coffee himself.

CHOCK FULL O' NUTS: THE HEAVENLY COFFEE

Coffee is supposed to be chock full of beans. Why, then, is one national brand of supermarket coffee called Chock Full O' Nuts? The answer is simply because that company started out as a nut business.

Sometime in the mid-1920s, William Black sold nuts from a pushcart on the streets of New York City. Later he sublet a space in a Times Square drugstore. When the Depression hit, sales of luxury items such as nuts slowed. So Black turned his nut stand into a coffee counter, baking his nuts into loaves of date nut bread, slathering it with cream cheese and selling it with hot coffee.

By the 1940s, Black was operating a whole chain of restaurants in New York, New Jersey and eastern Pennsylvania based on this concept. Because Black insisted his restaurant operators throw out any pot of coffee more than 15 minutes old, the restaurants became especially famous for their fine coffee. In the early 1950s, Black began putting the coffee in cans and selling it in supermarkets.

The well-known Chock Full O' Nuts advertising jingle was written in 1953 to showcase the talents of Black's then wife, Jean Martin, a former big band singer. To emphasize its high quality and justify its higher cost, the original lyrics said, "A better coffee a Rockefeller's money can't buy." When the Rockefellers objected, it was changed to "a millionaire's money can't buy."

The last Chock Full O' Nuts restaurant closed in 1991, but the coffee perks on.

SANKA: THE DOCTORS' CHOICE

There are those who argue that the only good reason to drink coffee is for the effects of the caffeine. But if Dr. Ludwig Roselius were alive today, he would probably disagree.

Roselius, head of a large European coffee business based in Bremen, Germany, had long searched for a way to remove caffeine from coffee without ruining its flavor. After years of unsuccessful experiments, a shipload of his company's coffee was deluged with seawater during a storm in 1903. Ruined for consumption, he turned it over to his researchers to experiment with. They found that the brine-soaked coffee beans reacted differently to their experiments. This bit of information gave Roselius an idea for a new series of tests eventually leading to a process that removed 97 percent of the caffeine without unduly injuring coffee flavor. When Roselius introduced his new product in France, he called it Sanka—a contraction of the French phrase *sans caffeine* or "without caffeine."

Sanka was introduced in the United States in 1923 and purchased by General Foods nine years later. A *New Yorker* cartoon of that time poked fun at the new product. Titled "Annual Banquet of the Sanka Coffee Corporation," it shows people at a table all sound asleep.

In 1946, Instant Sanka was introduced, and for many years, Instant's little orange-and-brown single-serve packets were synonymous with decaffeinated coffee in restaurants throughout the land. Still, the overall market for decaffeinated coffee was small and its consumers old.

Then came the health boom of the 1960s, when Sanka's total share of the coffee market almost doubled. Between 1977 and 1982, consumers were reminded of the health benefits of drinking Sanka-brand decaffeinated coffee by actor Robert Young, implicitly drawing on his longtime television role as the kindly Marcus Welby, M.D.

Today there are new methods of decaffeinating coffee and brands that some people think taste more like regular coffee. (General Foods itself came out with Brim in 1973.) But there's at least one advantage to drinking Instant Sanka. The taste is so unmistakably not caffeinated, there's no danger of ever falling prey to a waiter's mistake and drinking the hard stuff by accident.

SALADA: TEA AND SAYINGS

At the start, the main thing that distinguished Salada tea from other brands was the blend of tea leaves it was made with. For many years, the majority of teas sold in America came from the Orient. But in 1892, a Canadian grocery salesman named Peter C. Larkin introduced a blend that included tea from Ceylon. He named it after an Indian tea garden, Salada.

In 1956, Salada advertising director John Colpitts came up with an idea that made his product even more special. As one of his tag lines would later explain it, "From a little spark... burst a mighty flame."

Colpitts knew that the vast majority of tea drinkers brewed their tea by the cup, and he wanted to give them something to think about while waiting the three to five minutes for the tea to steep. At first the company put tea-making tips on the tags, but one stating the superiority of making tea in teapots proved controversial (a situation that gave Colpitts intimate familiarity with the tag line, "If you want a place in the sun, you have to have a few blisters"). So he switched to printing aphorisms. They were humorous ("To avoid that run-down feeling, cross streets carefully"), inspirational ("Triumph is just *umph* added to *try*") or philosophical ("When you have a fight with your conscience and get licked, you win"). Colpitts got some of the tag lines from employees, others from his own experience. For instance, when one of his sons became gravely ill, Colpitt tried to console his wife by saying, "Have faith. Nothing is as bad as it could be." And that became a tag line.

In the early 1960s, the company hired Stan Freberg to create a series of comic ads for Salada's tag lines or,

as he called them, "instant sayings." The campaign focused on the American Federation of Gypsies' strike against the Salada company for creating the tag lines and thereby taking fortune work away from them. The ad campaign culminated in a five-and-a-half minute radio mini-musical called "Woburn!" (after Salada's hometown of Woburn, Massachusetts).

Over the years, hundreds of people have written to Salada to say how the tag lines have influenced their lives. They certainly improved sales for Salada. Which just goes to show that as the tag line says, "True happiness is found in making others happy."

CELESTIAL SEASONINGS: BIG BUSINESS WAS NOT THEIR CUP OF TEA

For years Celestial Seasonings has dubbed its herbal teas "soothing teas for a nervous world." Employees of the Boulder, Colorado–based company needed to sip a lot of their own product in 1987 when, not long after telling some interested management employees that Celestial Seasonings was "not for sale," Kraft announced that it was selling Celestial to tea giant Lipton. Crying antitrust, the even tinier R. C. Bigelow tea company filed suit against Kraft.

While the case dragged on in the courts, Kraft itself became prey of the Phillip Morris Company. Having enough troubles of its own, Kraft decided to take the offer from Celestial Seasonings management. The day

the buyout was announced, Celestial's employees rose en masse for a standing ovation. And president Barney Feinblum sent two dozen red roses to Eunice Bigelow.

In understanding their euphoria at being divorced from one of America's largest food companies, it helps to know that Celestial Seasonings began with four hippies wandering around the valleys and canyons of the Rocky Mountains in the late 1960s collecting herbs to make their own tea.

Eventually Mo and Peggy Siegel, Wyck Hay and Lucinda Ziesing (whose nickname, Celestial, provided the company with its name) decided to sew their surplus into muslin sacks and sell it in local health food stores. Capitalizing the company with proceeds from the sale of a used Volkswagen, they moved sewing operations into a barn in Boulder. In the early days, President Siegel's secretary walked around barefoot, the vice president for human resources came to work in shorts and a T-shirt, and all employees got a free communal-style vegetarian lunch. Then, as now, there were never any time clocks, dress codes or executive parking spots, and employees got a $25 check on their birthdays.

With the introduction of a new tea blend called Red Zinger in 1972, the eccentric company began to take off. Once only a medicinal product, herbal tea boxes decorated with $15,000 pieces of artwork and New Agey sayings (at first, just President Siegel expounding his philosophies) fit the bill for a hip, upper-middle-class population concerned about the effect of caffeine on their increasingly healthy bodies. The revolution Celestial Seasonings thus created in the tea industry was bigger than anything since the Boston Tea Party (when herbal teas or Revolutionary Tea, as it was called, were drunk as a substitute for caffeinated English tea dumped in Boston Harbor).

Before long some of the big food companies began to take note of Celestial's success. When Siegel sold out to Kraft in order to go found something called the Jesusonian Foundation (a nonprofit group espousing philosophies about Jesus and life on other planets set forth in an ancient Urantia book), finance man Feinblum put off plans to leave the company to start a sprout farm in order to became Celestial's president.

The marriage between Kraft and Celestial Seasonings turned out to be nowhere near as happy as the one between oriental hibiscus flowers and wild rose hips of Red Zinger. Kraft didn't think the company was growing quickly enough; Celestial Seasonings executives were angry when Kraft refused to support Celestial's plans to pay Tour de France winner Greg LeMond to ride with the company-sponsored bicycle racing team.

Today Celestial Seasonings still sells more herbal teas than any other manufacturer—but the company does it its way. That includes using china and metal cutlery in the company cafeteria and putting their tea in 100 percent oxygen-bleached bags that have no paper tags or string. "It's better for the environment," says Siegel, who returned to the Celestial helm in August of 1991, bringing his "green" cleaning products business along as a Celestial subsidiary.

Where Kraft spent hundreds of thousands of dollars to test new Celestial products before putting them on the market, Celestial pays ladies' clubs and church groups to come in for tastings at $3.50 a head. The company also invites fans and friends to come to its visitors center, at company headquarters at 4600 Sleepytime Drive, Boulder, CO 80301-3292 (303-530-5300), to sample tea and take a peek into the huge production room. Since it's behind glass, shirts and shoes are not necessary.

POSTUM: THE CURE FOR CAFFEINE

"Is your yellow streak the coffee habit? Does it reduce your working force, kill your energy, push you into the big crowd of mongrels, deaden what thoroughbred blood you may have and neutralize all your efforts to make money and fame?" So asked an advertisement for Postum.

In 1895, years before Sanka was invented, C. W. Post sold a coffee substitute that he promised could solve virtually all those problems. Postum may be relegated to the sleepy side of the coffee aisle today, but it was the founding product of the company that became General Foods, one of the largest food companies in the world.

A Texas inventor and real estate developer, Post had lost his health and nearly all his money in a couple of disastrous business deals when he traveled to Battle Creek, Michigan to take the cure offered by Dr. John Harvey Kellogg (brother of soon-to-be cereal mogul W. W. Kellogg) at his famous sanitarium. Paying for his stay with a load of blankets from his failed mill, Post participated in Kellogg's regimen of exercise, hot baths and health food (including a Caramel Coffee made of bran, molasses and burnt bread crusts) for more than

10 months without improvement. When Post began to run out of money, he asked Kellogg if he could pay his bill by marketing his Caramel Coffee. Kellogg refused. But when Post moved out to live with a local Christian Science family, he began feeling better almost immediately.

News of Post's failure to thrive at Kellogg's and miraculous recovery elsewhere spread around town. Capitalizing on all the free publicity, Post opened his own sanitarium and called it La Vita Inn. La Vita did only mediocre business, but while running it Post developed his own coffee substitute, a mixture of wheat berries, bran and molasses. Later Kellogg would accuse Post of stealing his Caramel Coffee drink. But these types of poor man's coffees had been around since at least the Civil War. What distinguished Postum was the marketing and advertising savvy of its creator.

After investing $46.85 to buy a secondhand gasoline stove, a hand-operated peanut roaster and a coffee grinder, and $21.91 for ingredients, Post produced his first commercial batch of Postum on January 1, 1895. His "factory" was a horse barn on the La Vita property that's today used as a company infirmary. When grocers he approached expressed reservations about stocking the product, he told them they would not have to pay for it until it sold. He also promised to advertise in their local papers—a promise he was able to keep by convincing newspaper publishers and advertising agencies to give him space on credit. He wrote most of the ads himself, and they sent people running for Postum out of fear they could be affected by one of the hundreds of problems Post attributed to caffeine, including "lost eyesight," "coffee neuralgia," "poisonous alkalids," grouchy husbands and poor schoolwork. "Held back by coffee, this boy never had a fair chance," read one ad that showed the school dunce all alone in a classroom after school.

Another ad showed an acidy-looking liquid dripping from the spout of a coffeepot and read, "Constant dripping wears away the stone. Perhaps a hole has been started in you.... Try... Postum Food Coffee." Or, less threateningly, "If coffee don't agree—use Postum."

The advertising hit its mark. By 1901, Post saw profits of $385,000. He used much of that to pay for more advertising, explaining, "After you get it halfway down the customers' throat through the use of advertising, then they've got to swallow it."

Before long, Post would expand his food business to include several successful cereals (see *Grape-Nuts*). But his genius for business is perhaps best illustrated by the way he dealt with the Postum imitators that emerged with his success. Instead of changing his price or advertising more, Post himself created a new brand of cereal drink called Monk's Brew. Although it was in fact 100 percent Postum, he sold it for about a fifth of Postum's price. Monk's Brew undersold the other brands so dramatically that it put most of them out of business. Unsold packages of Monk's Brew that came back to the factory were dumped back into Postum boxes and sent out to be sold as Postum at the old price.

FROZEN FOODS

BIRDS EYE: THE FATHER OF FROZEN FOODS

Philosopher and scientist Sir Francis Bacon had the idea of freezing food way back in the 17th century, but died of exposure shortly after spending a cold winter's afternoon killing a chicken and stuffing it with snow.

Clarence Birdseye, on the other hand, not only survived his own experiments with freezing but lived to see millions of wax-paper-wrapped blocks of frozen food sold under his name.

Born in Brooklyn in 1886, Bob (nobody called him Clarence) Birdseye (he pronounced it BIRDS-ee) was the son of a judge who chose the more exciting life of an explorer, scientist and adventurer. In 1917 he went

to Labrador with his wife and baby son to trade fur and conduct a fish-and-wildlife survey for the U.S. government. While there he was impressed with how much fresher and more tender the Eskimos' fish and caribou meat tasted than similar foods that had been frozen and thawed back in the United States. Birdseye surmised this was because food froze more quickly in the frigid Arctic air than it did in freezers back home.

When Birdseye returned to the States in the early 1920s, he put his theory to test on some rabbits. After killing them, dressing them and packing them in boxes with jars filled with ice and salt, he sent them off in an insulated container to his sister. When she wrote that they were tasty, Birdseye began freezing steaks—and entertaining house guests by bouncing them on the kitchen floor.

Before long, he set up a company to sell frozen seafood wholesale. Through countless experiments in which he froze anything he could get from local fishermen (including sharks, small whales and once an alligator), he dis-

One of the demonstrators hired to introduce shoppers to Birds Eye products during the Postum Company's 40-week blitzkrieg in Springfield, MA in 1930 hard at work. Birds Eye products were then called "frosted foods," in part to distinguish them from the questionable quality cold storage foods consumers were already familiar with. Bird's Eye is a trademark of Kraft General Foods, Inc. Reproduced with permission.

covered the reason for the difference between fast and slow freezing: slow freezing forms large ice crystals, which destroy cell walls and the taste and texture of foods; fast freezing's smaller ice crystals do little damage.

In 1925, Birdseye invented the machine that would fast-freeze food and within two years was using it to freeze seafood. But sales were so poor that in 1929, Birdseye decided to sell his patents, methods and equipment to the Postum Company (later called General Foods).

A large company with a number of popular food products (including Baker's Chocolate, Jell-O and Maxwell House coffee), Postum was able to draw on its vast resources to convince the public that these were better frozen foods than the ones that had been produced by the old cold storage methods. One way they did this was by calling them "frosted" rather than frozen. Among the 27 initial varieties of Birds Eye Frosted Foods were raspberries, peas, spinach and haddock. (Birdseye said he didn't mind the splitting of his name as that's the way his ancestors had originally spelled it.)

The company started with a 40-week assault on supermarkets in Springfield, Massachusetts, installing frozen food cases free of charge to the grocers, handing out samples of the food and hiring nutritionists to speak about the products at women's club luncheons and home economics classrooms. But some foods defrosted in the distribution system. And sales were limited by the fact that hardly any consumers owned freezers. In 1933, General Foods decided to shift its frozen food sales efforts to hospitals and company cafeterias, where refrigeration was better and large numbers of people would get to try the food. This brought General Foods' Birds Eye division into the black.

But World War II is what really brought frozen foods into people's homes. With many women working, there was an increased demand for convenience foods. Canned goods needed to be rationed for their metal, so frozen food was a good alternative. When soldiers accustomed to being fed frozen foods returned from the war, Birds Eye's acceptance in the supermarket was secure.

And what of Clarence Birdseye? For a short while, he continued on as director of the Gloucester, MA laboratory, but soon he moved on to other projects: inventing a store window spotlight, harpooning whales and experimenting with dehydrating foods. Like Francis Bacon, Birdseye died from the effects of one of his research projects. In Peru, while trying to figure out how to make paper out of the agave plant, he suffered a heart attack attributed to high altitude.

STOUFFER'S HOMEY HAUTE CUISINE

Although there have been no studies to prove it, it seems likely that the steady rise in age at first marriage in this country is at least partly due to Stouffer's. Since this company elevated TV dinners to haute cuisine (albeit a distinctly American one of high-class chicken pies and macaroni and cheese), it has no longer been necessary to marry someone for their cooking ability. With all these single people eating Stouffer's, it is, in fact, becoming increasingly difficult to find a match who can cook at all.

Given the number of down-home foods in Stouffer's repertoire, it's not surprising to learn that the company began as a Cleveland restaurant that featured corned beef hash, baked beans, lasagna and Dutch apple pies homebaked by a woman named Mahala Stouffer. Mahala's first venture in the restaurant business was a stand-up Cleveland lunch counter that she opened in 1922 and ran with her husband, Abraham, until their 23-year-old son, Vernon, a Wharton Business School graduate, came home to work with them. He encouraged his parents to open a larger restaurant in Cleveland and before long, others in Detroit, Pittsburgh, New York City and a Cleveland suburb called Shaker Square. All were based on the original idea of serving high-quality homecooked meals at fair prices.

Sometime in the 1950s, orders-to-go at the chain's Shaker Square restaurant, situated right near a subway station, soared. Restaurant manager Wally Blankinship decided to try freezing some of the most popular meals and selling them at a retail store next door to the restaurant. The venture was so successful that in 1954, the Stouffers decided to open a frozen foods processing plant on Cleveland's Woodland Avenue and sell the same dinners in supermarkets.

Among the 25 products initially featured were macaroni and cheese and spinach soufflé—still two of Stouffer's most popular regular Red Box entrées. In 1981, Stouffer's scored a major success with its Lean Cuisine line of low-calorie meals for the growing number of American dieters. In 1991, Stouffer's reformulated Lean Cuisine to meet new consumer concerns about fat, sodium and cholesterol and almost simultaneously introduced Homestyle entrées—comfort food in larger portions.

In 1992, Stouffer's sold all of its restaurant businesses and the original Shaker Square Restaurant closed. In its latter years that restaurant had been called Vernon's Pier East, after one of Stouffer's founders. But it served no food you would have recognized from the TV dinners.

SWANSON TV DINNERS: FROZEN IN TIME

In recent years food manufacturers have made valiant attempts to get people to call their upscale frozen foodstuffs "frozen dinners" or "frozen entrées." But most people still call them TV dinners, after the very first frozen dinner made by Swanson in 1954. The Swanson dinners' first cardboard box even looked like a TV, with a simulated wood-grain border and a picture of the food in the place where the screen would be.

No ads ever told people they should eat the dinners while watching TV—Swanson's intent was really just trying to create an association between the miracle of television and the miracle of a "heat and eat" meal. Consumers themselves turned them into natural companions. With all eyes glued to the TV, who

had time to cook anyway?

The Swanson Company was founded by Swedish immigrant Carl Swanson, who arrived in the United States in 1896 a nearly penniless 17-year-old with a sign around his neck that read, "Carl Swanson, Swedish. Send me to Omaha. I speak no English." In Omaha, where two of his sisters lived, Swanson worked days and went to school at night. In typical Horatio Alger style, he graduated from a job as a grocery clerk to a partner in a grocery wholesale business that eventually grew into the largest processor of turkeys in the United States.

After Carl's death his sons, Gilbert and Clarke, took up the idea of making frozen potpies, and later TV dinners, as a way to broaden the market for poultry beyond the holidays.

The very first TV dinner contained turkey, corn bread dressing and whipped sweet potatoes and cost 98 cents. But problems with the sweet potatoes turning watery precipitated an almost immediate switch to regular potatoes. The second dinner variety, fried chicken, sold quickly until consumers began to complain that it tasted like bananas. It turned out that a banana-scented yellow dye that was being used to decorate the TV dinner box cover was not being given enough time to dry. (Swanson ended up selling the whole lot of banana fried chicken to a food chain in Florida that said their customers actually preferred the new taste.) As these problems were ironed out and sales increased, the cost of the dinners dropped to as low as 69 cents.

But people didn't just buy the dinners because of the food and the price. The divided aluminum trays were also a draw—so much so that people wrote to the company asking if they could buy empty ones. Newlyweds and others without much money used them to make Christmas tree ornaments.

Now the only place you can find the tray is in the archives of the Smithsonian Institution's National Museum of American History. It was retired from general use in 1984 because it couldn't be used in the microwave. Although Swanson dinners are now outsold by the more upscale Stouffer's, Weight Watchers and Healthy Choice, there is still apparently a loyal audience for the Model A of frozen dinners, particularly for Salisbury steak and the original turkey and fried chicken dinners.

Trying to keep up with the health-conscious times, Swanson replaced the brownie in the fried chicken dinner with a fruit dessert in 1986 but reversed the decision in 1987 after a flood of consumer complaints.

MINUTE MAID: BING'S ORANGE JUICE

In 1942, the U.S. Army let it be known that it would be willing to offer a $750,000 contract to anyone who could come up with an orange juice powder that could be produced cheaply and in quantity. They were looking for something along the lines of what we know today as Tang.

Adapting an evaporation technique it had developed for penicillin to orange juice, the National Research Corporation had been able to concentrate the juice, hold it in cold storage and finally (but not without considerable difficulty) dry it. By 1945, NRC had the contract. But one hour after NRC company president John Fox had picked up plant financing from investors, the A-bomb was dropped on Hiroshima. With the war soon to be over, Fox realized he would have to find a new market for his orange powder.

To make some money while he was working out the kinks in drying, Fox decided to try selling off some of the frozen concentrate. Executives of the Henry Loudon advertising agency in Boston, a town famous for its Revolutionary War Minutemen, helped him come up with a name. Minute meant quick preparation, and Maid was a simple acknowledgment that women did most of the work in the kitchen.

The first truckload of frozen Minute Maid rolled out of the plant on April 15, 1946. Sales looked promising until a bumper crop of fruits and vegetables brought fresh produce prices crashing. Frozen foods had already developed a reputation for poor quality during the war, and now they also cost more than fresh.

To save his company, Fox began an aggressive strategy of advertising and promotion that included sponsoring a 15-minute, five-day-a-week Bing Crosby show on radio. Crosby's popularity and easygoing image were just what was needed to help people overcome their fears of the freezer. One print ad featured a picture of Bing saying he himself would refund the price of their first can of Minute Maid. Crosby sang and talked about the juice so much on radio that most people assumed he owned the company. Although this wasn't true, Crosby did receive 20,000 shares of the company at the start of his contract. And in January of 1950, when a new Minute Maid division office was set up in Los Angeles, Bing Crosby was named president.

Other early ads stressed the amazingly good taste of frozen orange juice ("What! Orange groves on Long Island? You'll think so when you taste Minute Maid..."), its convenience ("Never Again Have to Squeeze Another Orange") and its nutritional superiority to fresh. The latter claim was based wholly on the fact that Minute Maid offered "¼ more juice for the same money than oranges squeezed at home" and therefore "¼ more healthful juice" and "¼ more body-building minerals."

By the time 30 other frozen orange juice brands were crowding the market in 1949, Minute Maid was number one. To help maintain that lead, Minute Maid redesigned its label. From featuring a white band on a field of oranges, the can became predominantly black with the trademark orange drop. In 1964, it was heresy to put black on a food product, but it stood out in the all-white frozen food cabinets and signified quality and class (an association new owner Coca-Cola wanted to maintain to justify Minute Maid's slightly higher price).

The quality theme resounded in Minute Maid's 1968 advertising slogan, "The Best There Is." Figuring that Bing Crosby was about the best there was when it had come to company advertising, Minute Maid officials asked him to return as product spokesman. Crosby was reluctant to appear on camera but agreed to be the voice-over announcer if his children could star and thus gain some television exposure.

For four years, Kathryn Crosby and the kids were shown making and drinking Minute Maid in their home. In one ad in the fourth year, viewers got a glimpse of Bing driving by in his golf cart. The acting bug reawakened, Bing starred in the ads alone from then until his death in 1977. In 1978, TV viewers got closure when Kathryn and her now grown-up kids did a commercial postmortem standing next to a portrait of Crosby.

COOL WHIP: DREAM OF A CREAM

In early 1965, through consumer testing, General Foods discovered great interest in a whipped-cream-like product that didn't spoil as quickly as the real thing, cost as much, have as many calories or have to be whipped. Food scientists set to work. Within six months, they had bested Mother Nature with a creation meeting all these specifications. It was named Cool Whip.

Cool Whip was invented at the tail end of the post-war convenience craze. A generation of women who had gone to work during the war were now unwilling to stay home fussing over meals. Industrialization and the space race had created an uncritical fascination with technological innovation, good or ill. So what if the "new" whipped cream had no cream in it? The most important thing was that it tasted sweet, stayed stiff and didn't leave you thinking you needed an arm sling from whipping the way its dried, non-dairy-topping predecessors had.

General Foods tested its new product in one city known to use a lot of whipped cream (Seattle, Washington) and another where processed toppings were king (Buffalo, New York). With the help of advertising and some recipe suggestions, Cool Whip became the number one processed topping in both cities in only three months. With its national introduction, waves of Cool Whip swept over the land, first as a substitute for whipping cream on pies and Jell-O but eventually as an ingredient in recipes (layered Jell-O desserts, fluffy fruit salads and imitation mousses—see recipe below) beyond the staying power of any real cream-based concoction.

Cool Whip lasts up to a year in the freezer and two weeks in the refrigerator (although its lifetime can be extended by multiple refreezing). Even after the Cool Whip is all gone, the memory of it lives on in its neat, resealable, white plastic storage container.

Mousse in a Minute

2 ¼ cups cold milk
1 package (6 oz.) instant pudding or pie filling, any flavor
1 ½ cups Cool Whip, thawed

Pour cold milk into small mixer bowl. Add pudding mix. Beat at lowest speed of electric mixer until well blended, 1 to 2 minutes. Fold in whipped topping and spoon into dessert dishes. Garnish with additional whipped topping if desired. Makes 4 cups or 8 servings.

Add it all up and it shouldn't be hard to understand why, even in the health conscious 1990s, Market Research Institute figures show one out of three American households still buying one of the three varieties of Cool Whip (regular, light or real cream) regularly.

ESKIMO PIE: CANDY AND ICE CREAM RUB NOSES

In an age of Dove Bars and Häagen-Dazs, an Eskimo Pie might not seem like enough of a treat anymore. But even those who prefer premium brands owe a debt of gratitude to the simple chocolate-covered block of vanilla ice cream wrapped in foil. Before the Eskimo Pie, no product had put ice cream and candy together.

The Eskimo Pie was inspired by an indecisive schoolboy who went into Christian Nelson's ice cream and confectionery store in Onawa, Iowa, one day in 1920. First the boy asked for a candy bar. Then he asked for an ice cream sandwich instead. Then he decided what he really wanted was a marshmallow-nut bar.

Nelson had seen indecisive young customers before. But this time, it gave him an idea. If the boy wanted both chocolate candy and ice cream, why wasn't there an ice cream treat to fulfill both these desires?

This thought started Nelson on a year of experimentation with chocolate and ice cream. He spent months trying to get chocolate to stick to ice cream, until a candy salesman tipped him off to what the big candy manufacturers used for their coatings: cocoa butter. Before long Nelson found that a certain combination of cocoa butter, sugar and chocolate heated to 80 or 90 degrees would adhere to ice cream and harden if immediately frozen. He called his new treat the I-Scream Bar and advertised it with the phrase, "I scream, you scream, we all scream for the I-Scream Bar" (a hit Tin Pan Alley song later showed up with almost the same name).

But Russell Stover, the marketing man Nelson hooked up with to take the product national, didn't like the name. After sending Nelson and Stover's sister, Mrs. Lem Jones, to the Omaha Public Library to collect a list of several hundred words pertaining to cold, Stover held a dinner party at which the name "Eskimo" was chosen. Stover added the word "Pie" to make con-

Christian Nelson invented the Eskimo Pie and also the circa 1929 thermos-based forerunner of the portable freezer to encourage impulse sales of his chocolate-covered ice cream treat. The dry-ice-filled Eskimo Jug rested on the backs of three little metal Eskimos and bore the slogan, "Bracing as a Frosty Morning."

sumers associate the new treat with a tasty and familiar dessert. Stover also had the idea of wrapping the bar in shiny Reynolds aluminum foil.

R.S. Reynolds' United States Foil Company made plenty of money on the Eskimo Pie craze, and when the cost of defending Nelson's Eskimo Pie patent from hundreds of knockoffs threatened to throw Nelson's company over, it was Reynolds Nelson turned to for help. (By this time Stover had bailed out and gone to Denver with the $30,000 Nelson paid him to start the first of the Russell Stover chain of chocolate candy shops and products.) Although Reynolds bought the Eskimo Pie Company, Nelson was made a principal stockholder and given lifetime royalties of a fraction of a cent for every Eskimo Pie sold.

It was more than enough to retire on, but instead, Nelson went on to pioneer the use of dry ice in ice cream shipping and to invent a thermos-based forerunner of the portable freezers that stand at the checkout counters of almost every convenience store in America, tempting consumers with Dove Bars, Popsicles and yes, even Eskimo Pies. Christian Nelson collected royalties on sales of Eskimo Pies until his death in 1992 at age 98. Russell Stover didn't do so badly either.

POPSICLE®: NOSTALGIA ON A STICK

Sure, those newfangled frozen 100 percent juice bars taste good, but how many of them can honestly claim to be part of Americana in the same way as Popsicle?

Proof is with the Eighth Air Force unit, which during World War II chose Popsicle as its symbol of American life while other units were fighting for Mom, apple pie, baseball or a favorite pinup girl.

Feelings for Popsicle continued to run so strong that when it was reported that U.S. Marine commander "Chesty" Puller reprimanded some men he spotted nibbling on the frozen treat, there was such a public outcry that Washington not only reversed Puller's decision; the politicians decided that Popsicle should be served at Marine mess at least once a week. All this fuss over a food an 11-year-old boy created by accident.

As the story goes, 11-year-old Frank Epperson left a mixture of powdered soda pop mix and water on his back porch with the stirring stick still stuck in it.

After a night of record cold, Epperson went out to find a stick of frozen soda water, which he showed to his school friends. But it wasn't until Epperson was all grown up and running a lemonade stand at an amusement park in Oakland, California that he realized the commercial possibilities of the accidental invention he first called Epsicle (combining the first two letters of his own name with "sicle") but soon changed to Popsicle (because his kids called them Pop's cycles). The realization was prompted in part by hearing of Harry Burt's Good Humor ice cream on a stick. When Epperson went to patent the Popsicle in 1923, Burt protested. But the two eventually reached a compromise where Epperson agreed to make only sherbet or water ice products, and Burt, only ice-cream-based ones. (Years later the companies these two men founded would merge to become Gold Bond–Good Humor Ice Cream Inc.).

Popsicle popularity grew with the boom in large-scale sports games and concerts in the 1920s; Popsicle bars were hawked by vendors at many of these events. During the Depression, the Twin Popsicle hit the market. It sold for a nickel but savvy merchants divided them up and sold them for three cents each. With the 1950s movement to the suburbs and the decline of the corner store, Popsicle came out in multi-packages for supermarket sales.

Originally manufactured in individual test tubes, then frozen in two separate steps, Popsicle bars today are made in only about eight minutes. First liquid formula is injected into molds that sit in a large tub of icy brine. Then the stick is inserted. Finally the hardened Popsicle is pulled from the mold and dipped in water. That's what gives them their glossy shine.

Although hundreds of exotic flavors have been tried, the best-selling ones are the highly unsophisticated cherry, orange and grape.

BEN & JERRY'S FUNKY COMPANY

For many years the highlight of the company's annual meeting—a picnic held on the grounds of its Waterbury, Vermont, headquarters—was the moment when founder Jerry took a sledgehammer to a cinder block that was resting on partner Ben's stomach (a trick that Jerry learned while taking a course on carnival techniques at Oberlin College).

This is how the fun-loving Ben & Jerry run their ice cream business:

- Seven and a half percent of pretax profits are donated to charities;

- Product packaging looks like it was designed by somebody from *Mad* magazine;

- In place of national advertising, Ben & Jerry's goodwill trucks travel the country, giving away free ice cream;

- The grand prize in a company-sponsored "Lick Winter" contest was a trip to Florida to have dinner with Jerry's parents;

- They put all-natural ingredients in all products except Heath Bar Crunch. (The explanation printed on every package? "We love [Heath Bars] so much we just can't help ourselves.")

Ben Cohen and Jerry Greenfield never set out to become the makers of one of the best-selling brands of superpremium ice cream in the country. Friends since high school, Ben was a Colgate University dropout who was teaching potterymaking and Jerry was a medical school reject working as a lab technician when they decided to move to a quiet college town in Vermont and go into business together. Their first choice was a bagel restaurant, but when they found out how much bagel-making equipment cost, they decided to try homemade ice cream instead.

Armed with little more information than what they learned from a five-dollar Pennsylvania State University ice cream making correspondence course, they bought an old rock salt ice cream maker, rented an abandoned gas station just outside of the University of Vermont in Burlington and decorated it with a lot of cartoony graphics of ice cream cones. There was a pianist to entertain people waiting in line, movies shown on the side of the building on summer evenings and when they ran out of ice cream, a posting of the international sign for no ice cream (a red circle containing an ice cream cone with a line drawn through). Today more than a quarter of a million people visit Ben & Jerry's Rte. 100, Waterbury factory (802-244-5641) annually, making it the most popular tourist attraction in the state.

Besides being fresh, what makes their ice cream different is the candy mix-ins and its much denser consistency (a gallon of Ben & Jerry's Heath Bar Crunch still weighs 6½ pounds, or about two pounds more than the typical nonpremium). Then, of course, there are the funky names: Chunky Monkey for a banana ice cream, nut and chocolate chunk combination, and Cherry Garcia, in honor of rock star Jerry Garcia because Ben and Jerry used to be Deadheads.

The pair began packaging their ice cream in pints and selling it to local supermarkets mainly as a way to keep solvent during the slow winter months. When they tried to expand their supermarket sales into southern New England, they found few distributors willing to take them on. Ben & Jerry's eventually decided that competitor Häagen-Dazs had told them to stay away from Ben & Jerry's or risk losing the Häagen-Dazs account. Ben & Jerry's promptly sued Häagen-Dazs, which is owned by Pillsbury. Ben and Jerry also set up a picket line in front of Pillsbury headquarters in Minneapolis (it consisted of just Jerry), printed up bumper stickers and T-shirts that said, "What's the Pillsbury Doughboy Afraid Of?" and set up a Doughboy hot line where people could call to get a kit of information to help them write letters of protest to Pillsbury chairman W. H. Spoor. People also sent letters of support to Ben & Jerry's, many of which mentioned their favorite flavor of ice cream (one was signed "Helene 'Dastardly Mash' Jones"). Some distraught children even offered to form Doughboy hit squads.

As it turned out, this sort of desperate action never became necessary. Häagen-Dazs relented and settled out of court. To most ice cream fans it was like watching Mom and Dad fighting. Different companies with different styles that don't get along—but we love them both. We're glad it's over so we can pig out in peace.

They may be big business men, but on the covers of Ben & Jerry's ice cream pints Ben Cohen (left) and Jerry Greenfield still look like the pair of Vermont hippies they were when they opened their first ice cream shop.

NOBODY DOESN'T LIKE THE REAL SARA LEE

As a youngster, Sara Lee was embarrassed by all the attention she received as namesake of her father's frozen dessert company, but today she hawks Sara Lee products on television and in personal appearances.

Yes, Virginia, there is a real Sara Lee. She was nine years old in 1949, when her father, Charles Lubin, decided to name his new company after her because he said, "Sara Lee sounds wholesome and American."

Lubin had owned and operated a chain of retail bak-

eries in Chicago for 14 years when he decided to expand distribution of his premium baked goods into supermarkets. Sara Lee products were sold only to grocery stores in greater Chicago until Lubin met a Houston businessman who fell in love with his cheesecake while in the Midwest and asked if they could be shipped to him. Lubin refused, citing spoilage problems. But the businessman wouldn't take no for an answer. Nudged by this man's weekly phone calls asking, "Where's the cheesecake?" Lubin figured out a way to take the technology that had been used to freeze vegetables and juice and apply it to baked goods.

By 1953 the Texan had his cheesecake, Lubin had a way to ship his products all over the country and the supermarket industry had a whole new category of frozen foods. Soon the cheesecake was joined by all-butter pecan coffee cake and the company's all-time best-seller, all-butter pound cake.

As the Sara Lee products became better known, Lubin got a kick out of introducing people to the real Sara Lee. Recently a grown-up Sara Lee Lubin recalled, "Whenever we went out to eat, he'd want to go in the kitchen and see who the chef was, and the baker. And he'd want me to go with him. That way he'd be able to say, 'This is Sara Lee.' But I would hate it. A lot of times I wouldn't go, but then he'd bring the chef out. I was mortified."

By age 19, Sara Lee was married and living in Boston and only her closest friends knew of her connection to their favorite cheesecake. It was only after her father had died and Sara Lee had divorced that she decided to become involved with the company, appearing in ads and at company functions, supermarkets and Sara Lee factories.

Today Sara Lee Bakery is one of the largest users of dairy products in the country (one of its plants, located in Rock Island, Illinois, is devoted totally to cracking eggs). Butter is interspersed with rolled yeast dough to make Sara Lee croissants and coffee cakes with 108 layers of flaky pastry. Sara Lee Lubin says people often stop to tell her how much they love her cheesecake or how her brownies once got them through a particularly dreary Saturday evening.

This tends to lend credence to the company's famous advertising slogan, "Nobody doesn't like Sara Lee." Indeed, in recent years Liza Minnelli has taken to singing a musical tribute to her Highness of frozen desserts written by "Cabaret" creators John Kander and Fred Ebb. But, banana cake and spice muffins aside, Sara Lee Lubin says, "I've certainly had a few people over the years who didn't like me!"

LENDER'S BAGELS: MANNA TO TRANSPLANTED MANHATTANITES

For many years, New Yorkers transplanted to Peoria, Illinois or Cheyenne, Wyoming could only view bagels as they did their first kiss or their last paycheck: longingly and from a distance. All that changed in 1962, when the Lender family of New Haven, Connecticut, began freezing bagels and selling them to supermarkets around the country. To Jews living outside metropolitan areas, Lender's bagels were manna in the wilderness.

Harry Lender opened his Connecticut bagel bakery in 1927, the first outside New York City, shortly after immigrating to America from Lublin, Poland. At first, his products were distributed through Jewish delicatessens and bakeries and sold to Jewish customers in New Haven. Gradually, though, word of Harry's delicious "roll with a hole" spread to the Italian, Irish and Russian enclaves in the neighborhood and local grocery stores serving those communities began carrying them.

But there was a problem. Bagels not sold the first day would quickly grow stale. Flash freezing proved effective, and soon frozen Lender's bagels were being shipped everywhere, turning Murray and Marvin Lender, sons of Harry and inheritors of the business, into bagel ambassadors.

To help fulfill that mission, the Lenders have colored bagels green on St. Patrick's Day and given them away to government officials and charities every year since 1955. In 1983, after hearing that the White House was encouraging business support for the Summit of Industrialized Nations, they paid two artists to paint and decorate stale bagelettes to resemble the participants. (Although the CIA initially made noises about wanting to cut the bagel heads apart to check for explosives, they eventually agreed to accept the diorama intact.) A full-time company artist churns out similar tributes to visiting celebrities and honored company employees.

The success of their efforts is reflected in company growth—from six family employees to more than 600; one factory to four. In 1984 Kraft purchased Lender's as a companion for Philadelphia Cream Cheese, and Murray and Marvin devoted themselves to serving fresh bagels at H. Lender and Sons restaurants in suburban Orange and Hamden, Connecticut. Murray also does an occasional ad for Kraft.

There are those who say that Lender's frozen bagels aren't the real thing. They say the outer crust isn't crunchy and the inner one is more soft than chewy, the way it should be. They might as well criticize a Twinkie for not being a homemade cake. In any case, for the 75 percent of Americans who never buy bagels, and for those who live without access to fresh, Lender's defines the food.

TOTINO'S PIZZA: BLESSED BE THE CRISP CRUST

When Rose and Jim Totino went looking for a business loan so they could open a pizza parlor in 1952, many Americans had never tasted the Italian pie. Well aware of this fact, Rose Totino delivered a freshly baked pizza to the bank officer assigned to their case. He liked the pizza but apparently forgot exactly what it was he had eaten. For when he went to tell them the news that the loan had been granted, he asked to speak to Mr. and Mrs. Pizza.

Armed with the bank's $1,500, the "Pizzas" opened Totino's Italian Kitchen, a small restaurant located in northeast Minneapolis featuring a thin-crust pizza from Rose's mother's recipe. People loved her pizza, and the business prospered, although the Totinos were often too tired to count money. "We'd just put it in a paper bag and write the date on it. The next morning we'd pay the milkman, the bread man, the meat man and all the bills. We'd always have some money left. I'd say, 'Look, Jim, I guess we're profitable,'" Rose has recalled.

The Totinos planned to save $5,000 a year for 10 years and then retire. But in 1962, they decided instead to use the $50,000 to begin a frozen Italian entrée business, with the goal of making frozen pizza as soon as they could afford the equipment to bake their own crusts. But the entrées did not do well. In fact, they did so badly that by the end of the first year, the Totinos were $150,000 in the hole.

One day in the midst of this crisis, Rose was driving to work when she turned on the radio to a college radio station and heard a Presbyterian preacher giving a talk on how God can help in times of trouble. Rose immediately pulled off the road and began to pray.

Not long afterward, the Totinos learned of a company that could supply them with prebaked pizza crusts and secured a $50,000 Small Business Administration loan. The Totinos were back in business—but this time, making a frozen version of the product that had built their local reputation. Six months after beginning production, they were out of debt and experiencing sales growth of 35 percent per year.

In 1970, business had grown to the point that the Totinos needed to build a new factory. Shortly afterward, Jim was diagnosed as having Parkinson's disease and the Totinos began to think about selling out. In 1975, Minneapolis-based Pillsbury made them an offer of $16 million. But Rose told them she wanted $20 million. When a Pillsbury executive asked how she came up with her figure, Rose said, "It's God's will." So they gave it to her.

After taking over, Pillsbury set to work on making Totino's pizza crust taste more like the one Rose made in her restaurant and less like cardboard—a common complaint of frozen pizza consumers. In 1978, Totino's new Crisp Crust Pizza became America's best-selling brand of frozen pizza—that is, until Jeno's figured out how to imitate what Pillsbury had done. (In 1981, Pillsbury also acquired Jeno's—and began marketing it as a snack-time pizza so the two brands wouldn't steal customers from each another.)

Jim Totino died in 1981. But Rose became Pillsbury's first woman vice president. Her duties have included advertising and public relations for her namesake brand as well as giving the invocation at corporate events such as the Bake-off contest and Pillsbury's annual meeting. At the 1980 annual meeting, she spoke of God's benevolence over company and country, then stepped away from the microphone. A few moments later she returned to the podium. "Lord, I forgot to thank you for crisp crust," she said, to shareholder laughter and cheers.

Totino's Italian Kitchen, 532 Central Avenue NE, Minneapolis (612-379-9105), is still owned by Rose and still serves a nonfrozen version of her crisp-crust pizza.

SNACKS

A Chip Off of Old Herman Lay

Potato chips were invented by native American chef George Crum of Saratoga Springs, New York as a way to get revenge on a disgruntled restaurant customer. Commodore Cornelius Vanderbilt had sent his french fries back to the kitchen one night in 1853 complaining that they were too thick. Meaning to annoy, Crum cut Vanderbilt's next batch paper thin. To Crum's surprise, Vanderbilt loved them. And so did lots of other customers at his restaurant.

Because of the work involved in peeling and slicing potatoes by hand, potato chips remained a restaurant specialty until the invention of the mechanical potato peeler in the 1920s. After commercial production had begun, it took a traveling salesman named Herman Lay to make potato chips a staple grocery store item in the South and eventually all over the country.

In 1932, after having worked for a time as a lumberjack, a wheat harvester and a jewelry salesman, Lay paid $100 to buy the Nashville, Tennessee, warehouse of Atlanta's Barrett snack food firm and began selling potato chips from the trunk of his 1928 Model A. By 1934, his selling territory had expanded to include six routes, and he was doing so well that when his Atlanta supplier got into financial difficulty, he was able to buy him out. Naturally he changed the name of the company to Herman W. Lay.

In 1944, Lay's became one of the first snack food companies to advertise on television. The company's spokes-spud was Oscar the Happy Potato, who made his debut singing, "I'm a treat, full of zip! I'm a Lay's potato chip!"

A year later, Lay entered into a franchise agreement with Fritos maker Elmer Doolin, securing the right to make and sell Fritos in the Southeast. In 1961, the agreement turned into a merger that was worked out

Oscar the Happy Potato became Lay's Potato Chip spokespud in 1944, representing the company on packaging, advertisements and this parade float.

by four men (two from each company) at a secret meeting held in a motel in Jackson, Mississippi. The new company was called Frito-Lay. When common stock for the company appeared on the New York Stock Exchange for the first time, the company celebrated by releasing limited quantities of blue-hued potato chips. When Pepsi merged with Frito-Lay in 1965, Herman Lay was the new company's biggest single stockholder and chairman of the board.

As a big international company, Frito-Lay sells Lay's all over the world. In Mexico, Lay's are known as Sabritas; in Spain, Matutano; in Australia, Thins; in Canada, Dulac's; and in Korea, Poca Chips. But Americans eat more potato chips than any other people, and the bag they reach into most often is the yellow-netted Lay's.

A 1964 to 1968 Lay's potato chip ad campaign gave testimony to its addicting quality. "Betcha can't eat just one," comic actor Bert Lahr taunted viewers in the guise of Julius Caesar, the devil and Eve (of Adam and). At the 1964 New York World's Fair, Lahr was continually harassed by groups of children who followed him around with bags of chips, saying, "Betcha can't eat just one!" After Lahr died in 1967, Buddy Hackett was hired to deliver the newly revised line, "No Buddy can eat just one."

In fact, judging from Lay's current production schedule, Americans actually eat close to 7 million pounds worth of potatoes in the form of Lay's potato chips each and every day.

PRINGLES AND THE POTATO CHIP WAR

These days, the cardboard tubes of prefabricated Pringles are only one of several options offered the potato chip eater. As options go, it is one of the less popular, selling only about half as much as ridged chips. But when fabricated chips like Pringles were first introduced, they nearly caused civil war in the potato chip industry.

Within 60 years of their invention by George Crum, potato chips were a wildly popular national snack. Consumers had two major complaints about them, however: they broke too easily and got stale too quickly. In 1969, General Mills and Procter & Gamble both thought they had the answer: a "newfangled" potato chip not made from a sliced potato like traditional potato chips but from potatoes that had been cooked, mashed, dehydrated and reconstituted to form a potato dough. The dough in turn could be cut to a uniform size and shape and packaged in break-proof, life-extending, oxygen-free containers. General Mills called their version Chipos; P&G, Pringles. Both called them potato chips.

Members of the Potato Chip Institute, a trade association, were appalled. To that organization, potato chips meant one thing and one thing only: sliced potatoes fried crisp in oil. As far as it was concerned, General Mills and P&G were engaging in deceptive business practices calling these new foods potato chips, not to mention unfairly taking advantage of the millions of dollars real potato chip manufacturers spent on advertising. As General Mills was the first to make the "fake" potato chips nationally available, they were the first company the Potato Chip Institute brought to court over the issue. Meanwhile P&G began test marketing Pringles.

When the Potato Chip Institute lost their court battle with General Mills, they asked the Food and Drug Administration for its ruling on what could and could not be called potato chips. While awaiting the decision, dozens of new fabricated chips came out, including one from Frito-Lay, which had joined the association's suit against General Mills but apparently wanted to hedge its bet. In a display of rare corporate humor, Pillsbury called its fabricated chip French Frauds.

In 1975, the FDA finally came out with its ruling: Any product not made from fresh potatoes would have to be clearly labeled "potato chips made from dried potatoes." But the ruling was not to go into effect until 1977. By then, it had become obvious that only a relatively small number of people wanted to eat snacks out of tennis ball cans. In the early '90s Pringles was the best-selling brand of fabricated chips—and losing $5 million in supermarket sales per year.

Muncha Buncha Fritos

How many times have you stood at a deli counter, and while the clerk was making the sandwich, tried to decide whether or not to have a bag of snack chips with it? Elmer Doolin was in that situation one day in 1932, but his decision to spend an extra five cents on the bag of fried corn chips he saw sitting on the counter of that San Antonio café changed his life.

Although corn masa, or dough, had been used by the Mexicans of the Southwest to make bread for centuries, most Americans—like Doolin—had never tried anything like it.

Doolin's ice cream business was not doing so well and, he was looking for other opportunities. This product, called Fritos, tasted delicious. Through the proprietor of the café where he bought his sandwich, Doolin was able to find the maker of the chips, a Mexican eager to return to his native land.

His mother, Daisy Dean, hocked her wedding ring, and with the $100 she gave him Doolin bought the Mexican's recipe (based on an age-old one for Mexican corn dough bread), the Fritos name, 19 store accounts

In August 1934, the Frito Company offered a $10 prize to the route truck driver who sold more than $200 worth of Fritos and had the lowest percentage of stales for the month.

and the manufacturing equipment (a hand-operated potato ricer adapted for making corn chips). By night, Doolin and his mother made chips in her kitchen; by day, Doolin sold them out of the back of his Model T.

With a production capacity of only about 10 pounds an hour, Doolin could at first make only about two dollars a day profit on his business. Within a year, Doolin had come up with a more efficient press, which nevertheless had to be struck with a hammer when it came time to cut the strips of corn dough. He also began expanding his sales routes to other parts of the country, although he had to pay for at least one such trip, to St. Louis, by working as a night cook in a local restaurant. In 1945, Doolin met potato chip manufacturer Herman W. Lay and Lay agreed to help distribute Fritos.

From 1953 to 1967 the Fritos spokesperson was a little boy dressed up in a cowboy outfit and known as the Frito Kid. When the company switched to the Frito Bandito in 1968, Frito-Lay was accused of being anti-Mexican (ironic considering who first invented the product). The bandito was a smiling, mustachioed cartoon character who would stop at nothing to get his Fritos. Each ad began with the Frito Bandito stealing chips from someone and ended back in an average-looking house where an actor or actress would sneak a

hand into a bag and steal some chips. "Is there a Frito Bandito in your house?" the announcer asked as an animated mustache appeared across the person's lips.

Usually the bandito stole from supermarkets, pedestrians and picnickers, but one of the most memorable ads involved the Apollo astronauts. That commercial showed the astronauts landing on the moon only to find the Frito Bandito standing next to a parking meter waiting for them. "I ham the moon parking lot attendant," he said. "Now if you will kindly deposit one bag of cronchy Fritos corn cheeps for the first hour..."

The Mexican-American Anti-Defamation Committee criticized the commercials for spreading "the racist message that Mexicans are sneaky thieves." Frito-Lay denied any racist intent and even commissioned a poll that showed only 8 percent of Mexican-Americans objected to the Bandito. But Frito-Lay discontinued the ads anyway.

In addition to just munching a bunch of Fritos (a popular Fritos slogan from the late 1950s that was revived again in 1991), Southwesterners like to dress them up into a more substantial treat called the Walk-about. It's made by plopping chili, cheese and onions into an opened snack-size bag of Fritos and eating it with a spoon while walking around a fair or rodeo.

CRACKER JACK: A PRIZE OF A SNACK

Kids eagerly rip open the cardboard top of a box of Cracker Jack and rummage around in the golden brown nuggets of candied popcorn and peanuts to find the toy surprise. There isn't often anything in one of the paper envelopes that seems worth all the effort,

and yet, judging from the continuing popularity of the Cracker Jack snack; the search, the hope and the candy continue to have appeal.

F. W. Rueckheim was a German immigrant who came to Chicago in 1871 to help clean up after the Great Fire and stayed on to open a popcorn stand at 113 Fourth Avenue (now Federal Street). Business was so good that within two years, his brother was helping him sell a line of snack foods that had expanded to include peanuts, caramels, marshmallows and molasses taffy.

Sometime in the early 1890s, Rueckheim reasoned

that if customers enjoyed popcorn, peanuts and molasses taffy individually, why not all in one snack? The F. W. Rueckheim and Brother booth at the 1893 Columbian Exposition featured the treat.

Its name comes from a salesman's reaction to trying it for the first time. "That's a crackerjack!" the salesman said, using a then popular slang expression for something really good. Similarly the Cracker Jack slogan, "The more you eat, the more you want," came from a customer comment. By 1902, the candy was well known enough to appear in the Sears catalog without description. In 1908, its popularity as a ballpark treat was immortalized in the song "Take Me Out to the Ball Game" (the line was "Buy me some peanuts and Cracker Jack").

During World War I, the box acquired a patriotic red, white and blue color scheme and began featuring Sailor Jack and his dog. The boy was modeled after Rueckheim's eight-year-old grandson, Robert, who had a dog named Bingo. Sadly, Robert died of pneumonia shortly after the new box came out. A depiction of Sailor Jack is carved in the boy's tombstone, in St. Henry's Cemetery, Chicago.

But as well known as the baseball song and Sailor Jack may be, it's the toy surprises that really put Cracker Jack on the map. Looking back at Cracker Jack prizes provides a tiny but telling picture of American history. Baseball cards and score counters, metal whistles and tops were among the prizes featured in the very earliest years. Allied and Axis airplanes were featured in a set of cards designed to aid the amateur airplane spotter during World War II. One of the earliest plastic prizes, a figure of an old sea captain, was withdrawn from circulation in the late 1940s when anticommunists complained that it resembled Joseph Stalin. In recent years, there have been wiggle pictures to commemorate events at the 1984 Olympics and stickers depicting endangered wild animals.

Some of the older Cracker Jack prizes are valued in the hundreds of dollars. A very early cast metal horse and wagon commands $650. A full set of Cracker Jack baseball cards from 1914 is worth an amazing $17,000.

Today's prizes must meet basic safety standards and meet the approval of a rotating panel of children. Children most prefer prizes that they can easily understand and immediately play with. (Borden found this out the hard way when, after purchasing the company in 1964, it insisted on complex plastic puzzle prizes. They were abandoned after only a year.)

Samples of all 10,000 prizes ever issued were kept in a company vault until 1987 when they became the focus of the Cracker Jack Collection of historic prize displays, interpretive exhibits and games at the Center of Science and Industry, 280 E. Broad St., Columbus, Ohio 43215-3773 (614-228-2674).

A Jolly Kind of Popping Corn

In 1897 the Sears, Roebuck catalog advertised a 25-pound sack of popping corn on the cob for one dollar. What the ad didn't say but everyone knew is that the purchaser would be lucky if two thirds of the kernels on those cobs popped.

C. H. Smith was a Sioux City, Iowa, farmboy who had the idea that popcorn might be more popular if it were already shelled, free of debris and guaranteed to pop every time.

Only one year after he began producing just such a popcorn in the basement of his parent's house in 1914, Smith's American Pop Corn Company had sold more than 75,000 pounds of the stuff. No wonder he called his brand Jolly Time!

As the oldest name brand of popcorn on the market, the history and development of Jolly Time parallel the history and development of popcorn eating in America. At first, 40 percent of Jolly Time sales were still to the gaily painted, mobile popcorn wagons that sold popcorn on street corners across America. In the 1940s popcorn became almost synonymous with moviegoing—so much so that when television was invented in 1949 and movie-going declined, popcorn sales dwindled right along with it. It took a joint advertising campaign between the Popcorn Institute and Coca-Cola to convince Americans that Coke went with popcorn even if they happened to be at home. By mid-decade, a survey of TV owners showed that two out of three munched popcorn as often as four times a week.

The popping corn industry also experienced two peaks of growth during the 1980s: in 1980, when Weight Watchers made the treat "legal" for those on diets, and again in the mid-1980s, with the rise of cable TV movies, video tape rentals and microwave ovens.

In the early days, almost all the corn grown for popcorn was white. Today yellow kernels are preferred for their larger size (especially by movie concessionaires anxious to fill up cartons for less money) and because they look already buttered. Jolly Time is one of the few companies to still offer a white corn and although fans say it's sweeter, the company still sells about three times more yellow.

Consumers can also thank Jolly Time for inventing beer and soda cans. In 1925, after finding that some of its popcorn was drying out in cardboard boxes and thus not popping, Jolly Time hired the American Can Company to design the first airtight metal can. (The company subsequently switched to the less-expensive but just as effective cardboard can with a foil lining that Jolly Time uses today.)

Jolly Time is today still owned and operated by the Smith family (C. H.'s grandson is president, and two of his great-grandsons are vice presidents), and Jolly Time is the only national popcorn company not owned by or involved in nonpopcorn businesses.

POP STAR ORVILLE REDENBACHER

With his Gay Nineties hairstyle, bow tie and thick black glasses, Orville Redenbacher looks like some Hollywood casting agent's idea of a Midwestern hick. But unlike Rosie or Mr. Whipple, Redenbacher is as down home and real as the cornstalks from which his Gourmet Popping Corn originates.

As a youth, Redenbacher attended a one-room schoolhouse and grew popcorn as a 4-H project—selling it in local stores to make spending money. An early snapshot showing his clothes completely covered in 4-H ribbons offers proof of his success with this and other agricultural projects.

No one was particularly surprised, then, when Redenbacher turned down the chance to go to West Point in order to study agriculture at Purdue University. That school pioneered research on popcorn strains in the late 1920s, and it was a subject Redenbacher remained interested in, even while he worked as a county farm agent and managed an agribusiness. Finally, in 1952, he bought an agricultural business with college chum Charlie Bowman that they turned into the world's biggest producer of hybrid popcorn.

Convinced that a better popcorn could be developed than the ones they were selling to popcorn companies, Redenbacher spent a lot of time conducting cross-breeding experiments. In 1965, he found what he was looking for: a yellow corn that expanded almost twice as much as other brands and left almost no unpopped kernels (which Redenbacher called "shy ones"). But established companies, used to selling popcorn almost

A teenage Orville Redenbacher, stylish then as now, models a suit of 4-H ribbons he earned from his agricultural projects. One of them involved trying to grow a better variety of popping corn.

solely on the basis of price, didn't think consumers would be willing to pay for a premium brand.

Undaunted, Redenbacher dubbed his product Red Bow (after his trademark tie) and spent four years traveling the Midwest trying to sell it on his own. But he had only limited success until, in 1970, he consulted a Chicago marketing firm that advised him to put his face on the label and call his product Orville Redenbacher's Gourmet Popping Corn. At first Redenbacher balked at the idea. Kids used to tease him about his name, and he knew he was no Paul Newman.

But when he relented, Redenbacher discovered the wisdom of that advice. Redenbacher looked like just the kind of guy who had spent years obsessing to create the very best popcorn. Ads in which Redenbacher bellowed for his hard-of-hearing cow, spelled his name for a cop trying to give his popcorn wagon a ticket and hawked popcorn beside his grandson look-alike Gary were fun to watch. The ads also preempted people's objections to buying from such a, well, cornball, by playing into them. Orville Redenbacher was so out he was in.

By 1975, his product had become the nation's best selling. On the way to that achievement, his company helped to change popcorn from a generic product enjoyed largely in the South and Midwest to a highly competitive national industry with dozens of new companies and products (many of which, such as microwavable bags, Redenbacher innovated). But Orville Redenbacher still commands about half of all dollar sales.

In 1976, Redenbacher and Bowman sold their popcorn business to Hunt-Wesson and both became millionaires. Redenbacher now lives in a high-rise condominium overlooking the Pacific near San Diego, but, in a deal similar to the one Colonel Sanders had with Kentucky Fried Chicken, still makes personal appearances and advertisements for his popcorn.

YOU CALL THIS PEANUT, MISTER

They're not expensive like an almond, classy like a cashew or used in luxurious desserts like a macadamia. In fact, the peanut isn't a nut at all and almost all the peanuts grown for eating in the United States are of the single, same variety.

You need to think about this to realize the genius of Planters' Mr. Peanut. With his monocle, cane and top hat, Mr. Peanut elevates the humble peanut to a new level of dignity and class, lifting Planters peanuts above all other brands. He's also just plain fun to look at. Evidence is the hundreds of Mr. Peanut premiums people have paid good money to obtain.

And yet Mr. Peanut was not the product of a high-powered marketing firm or multi-million-dollar advertising campaign but of a 14-year-old schoolboy responding to a contest the company held in 1916. Antonio Gentile of Suffolk, Virginia won five dollars for his drawing of an animated peanut. A commercial artist spiffed him up with the fancy duds. On one of his early 1990's talk shows, David Letterman reported that Mr. Peanut's first name is Keith, that he belongs to a country club that doesn't admit pistachios, and that he was once arrested wandering New York's Port Authority at dawn chanting, "Eat Me!"

Planters itself was started by another Italian boy of 19. Amedeo Obici arrived in America when he was only 12, with no money, no knowledge of the English language and only a vague idea that he had an uncle who lived in Pennsylvania. Eventually, Obici found the uncle, and after working at his fruit stand in exchange for room and board, in 1896, the young man decided to move to Wilkes-Barre and go into business for himself. Although Obici also sold fruit, his pride and joy was a peanut roaster he had purchased for $4.50, then improved by adding pulleys that would automatically turn the peanuts to prevent scorching. He got the idea of adding salt or chocolate to some batches and soon was selling more peanuts than anything else.

In 1906, Obici abandoned fruits entirely and formed Planters Nut & Chocolate Company with fellow immigrant Mario Peruzzi. There was no good reason for the name Planters other than that they thought it sounded "important and dignified."

For most of the 1800s, well-to-do Americans had viewed peanuts as little more than animal feed. The only people who ate them were slaves and the poor. But the Union soldiers who had tasted peanuts, or "goobers," while fighting in the Civil War created new interest in the nut up north. At about the same time, showman P. T. Barnum began selling plain paper bags of peanuts at his circuses. (Shortly afterward the term "peanut gallery" began to be used for the remote seats in circuses, fairs and theaters where the poorest people usually sat.)

But it was Obici and Peruzzi who first got the idea to put peanuts in name-brand packages sealed for freshness. Obici and scientist George Washington Carver both helped to advance the idea of peanuts as a good, nutritious food: Carver because of the hundreds of uses he found for them through experimentation, Obici through an ad campaign that promoted Planters peanuts as a great "nickel lunch." In recent years, Planters products have expanded beyond Obici's nuts, peanut candy and peanut oil to include popcorn and puffed snacks—all still bearing the Mr. Peanut logo.

In 1991, Planters celebrated Mr. Peanut's 75th anniversary by honoring leaders in public education in six cities across the country. In addition to receiving money to donate to their favorite educational cause, the honorees got to place their footprints in wet cement alongside Mr. Peanut's peanut prints. In New York City this permanent tribute to the mayor's wife, Joyce B. Dinkins (who started a Reading Is Recreation program), and Mr. Peanut can be seen in front of the A & S plaza at the corner of Sixth Avenue and 33rd Street.

A SLIM BUT BEEFY SNACK

Bar food is governed by less demanding standards than almost anything else designed for human consumption. The food must be salty (to replace the salt lost in trips to the bathroom and to promote more drinking), and it must be substantial enough to stop someone from getting drunk too quickly. Subtle shades of flavor are usually lost on the inebriated palate and so aren't particularly important. All of which helps to explain the popularity of such food curiosities as pretzels, Cornnuts, Chex mix, sugared peanuts and the subject of this present inquiry, Slim Jim meat snacks.

Slim Jim is a direct descendant of cured beef products such as beef jerky and salt pork. Back in pioneer days, the most common way to keep a side of beef from spoiling was to salt it. Now refrigeration can do the trick—but only if you remember to pack a lunch and don't mind putting it at risk of theft in the company cafeteria refrigerator. Otherwise, Slim Jim is a convenient alternative. Like Kraft Handi-Snacks Cheez'n Crackers, Slim Jim is substantial food in a form every bit as durable and convenient as a package of cookies or potato chips. Slim Jims are also chewy enough to give your teeth and jaws a lot of exercise. For this reason, some see Slim Jim as the human equivalent of dog chew sticks.

What of the origin of the Slim Jim name and the package's depiction of a gentleman in a top hat? A spokeswoman for Slim Jim maker GoodMark Foods, Inc., says the name was chosen to fit the snack's long, slender shape. Slim Jim's tux and top hat might seem out of place in the bars where he's often consumed, but the company says the high-class outfit is merely meant to reflect the high quality of the product. The original Slim Jim logo showed the full figure of a man dressed in top hat and tails and leaning on a cane. But when new labeling regulations went into effect, the company scaled down the logo to simply the head of a gentleman tipping his top hat (which should give you some idea of the length of some of these ingredient lists).

Among the 30 varieties of Slim Jim are ones called Big Jerk, Giant Jerk and Super Jerk. Although the jerk in the names is meant to refer to the beef jerky the packages contain, it's easy to imagine more than one barroom brawl being started by someone who said it, not with flowers, but with a gift of one of these particular Slim Jims.

CANNED AND JARRED GOODS

A (Green) Giant Among Vegetable Canners

He presides over the vegetable freezer and canned vegetable sections of American supermarkets like some benevolent god or green Santa Claus, solving problems and then exiting with a hearty ho ho ho. But the first and most important good deed the Jolly Green Giant ever performed was to help a small food company from Le Sueur, Minnesota, grow into a giant among American vegetable processors.

In the early 1920s, a board member from the fledgling Minnesota Valley Canning Company returned from a trip to Europe with samples of a new variety of pea called Prince of Wales. Although wrinkled, oblong in shape and much larger than the Early June type the company was already canning, these peas were actually sweeter and more tender. When Minnesota Valley Canning's private label customers refused to buy the new peas, the company brought them out under their own label and with their own special name—Green Giant. Because the phrase was descriptive and, company attorneys advised, probably would not be entitled to trademark protection, they decided to put a picture of a giant on the label. That first Green Giant, borrowed from Grimm's Fairy Tales, wore a fur wrap and a scowl and wasn't even green (that was soon corrected despite the skepticism of one executive who protested, "Who ever heard of a green giant?").

When a young copywriter named Leo Burnett opened his own Chicago ad agency in the 1930s and got the Minnesota Valley Canning account, the Green Giant also gained height, a suit of leaves and such a friendly expression that Burnett began to call him Jolly. Burnett's ads established the Green Giant persona as a wise and caring guardian of the fields—a character so appealing to consumers that in 1950, Minnesota Valley Canning changed its name to Green Giant. In recent years the Giant has been joined by a cast of valley helpers and by a scene-stealing Little Green Sprout.

Incidentally, the cartoon Giant walked across the TV screen only once, during his 1959 TV debut. The consensus opinion was that he looked like a monster from a low-budget horror movie. That explains why he now mainly points, bends over or ho ho hos.

B&M®: The Beans of Portland, Maine

New England-style baked beans like B&M have their origins in a dish that was prepared by early American Indians. The native Americans would soak beans, place them in a clay pot with some deer fat, then cook them overnight in a hole in the ground lined with hot stones. The Pilgrims, whose religion prevented them from cooking after sundown on Saturdays, found the dish particularly useful to prepare ahead for Saturday dinner and Sunday lunch.

The custom of having baked beans for Saturday night supper persisted through later generations of New Englanders, who would save money on their own cooking fuel by dropping their pots of prepared beans off at the local bake shop to be cooked for a small fee. When they went to pick up their pots on Saturday evening, they would often buy a piece of the baker's fresh-baked brown bread to go with it.

At the turn of the century, some grocers and bakers started baking huge pots of brown beans and selling portions over the counter. Friend Brothers Bakery of Melrose, Massachusetts, began doorside delivery of

their baked beans and in 1918, to can them. In 1927, Burnham & Morrill, or B&M, a Portland, Maine, canning company then experiencing a decline in sales for two of its formerly popular corn and codfish cakes, decided to introduce its own New England-style baked beans. Friend Brothers sued for trademark infringement but lost when B&M was able to prove it made its beans from an old family recipe. (Interestingly, Friend's® and B&M are now both owned by Pet Incorporated.)

The B&M recipe includes salt pork, molasses, spices, sugar and tiny brown pea beans. Although not native to New England, the pea bean had been the favorite of New Englanders since the gold rush. At that time pea beans were used as ballast in New England ships returning from bringing supplies to California. Not the kind to throw anything away, the New Englanders ate the pea bean ballast and found them good tasting.

Today most commercial baked beans are produced using high speed processes. But the B&M factory in Portland (and one other in Buhl, Idaho) operates on the same principle as the bean-pot-filled ovens of New England bakeries of yesteryear. Instead of hundreds of tiny pots, several much larger ones are cooked in dry-heated brick ovens for about seven hours. When the wind is blowing, the smell of gently cooked spices and molasses—heavy, warm and meaty—can be picked up throughout the city.

Hunt—For the Best (in Tomato Sauce)

Open the cupboard of even a poorly stocked American kitchen and you can expect to see a can of Hunt's tomato sauce. These days tomato sauce is considered indispensable for making meat loafs, casseroles and stews—as much a kitchen basic as soup or coffee or butter.

This was not the case in 1940, and one smart businessman, Norton Simon, is largely responsible for the change. Simon was a young entrepreneur who purchased a defunct canning operation in Fullerton, California in 1934 and turned it into a company worth $9 million within a decade.

In 1943, Simon's business merged with Hunt Brothers Fruit Packing, a Hayward, California produce company started by the brothers Joseph and William Hancock Hunt that had a reputation for quality products. Although the new company took the Hunt name, Simon ran day-to-day operations. Given the compa-

nies' collective experience, a canned fruit or vegetable would obviously be the new company's main product—the only question was, which one to specialize in? Rather than try to compete with existing markets, Simon decided to create a national market for tomato sauce, a product then manufactured only regionally and used mainly by cooks of Italian descent. He did this by hiring home economists to create recipes with tomato sauce as a main ingredient and distributing them with one of the most extensive advertising campaigns ever attempted in the food industry.

Between 1946 and 1953, the metal red can appeared in full-page ads in newspapers, national magazines and billboards, each one featuring the company slogan "Hunt—For the Best." Millions of matchbooks also featured Hunt's on the covers and recipes inside. Sales of the sauce skyrocketed. By the 1960s, tomato sauce was such an accepted product that sales continued to grow even without advertising.

In 1981, Hunt-Wesson made the first significant change in the product in 40 years when, in response to consumer demand for a thicker sauce, they changed their processing technique and boosted the number of tomatoes in each can from four to four and a half.

Ragú: Recipe for Success

Giovanni and Assunta Cantisano might not have seemed very prosperous when they arrived at Ellis Island from their native Italy right after the turn of the century. But more important than the few suitcases full of clothes they carried with them was the knowledge in their heads. For it was their memory of a family recipe for spaghetti sauce that formed the basis of what would

eventually become a multi-million-dollar food business and a popular food in households around the country.

Giovanni's first business enterprise in America was as an importer of Italian pastas, wines and cheeses, first based in New York City, then later in Rochester, New York. Although the business was successful, the Cantisanos thought their own family spaghetti sauce—a blend of tomatoes, spices and cheese—was just as good as anything he was importing. In 1937, the Cantisanos began making the sauce in their own home and putting it up in mason jars to sell to friends and neighbors, and eventually to local stores as well. They called it Ragú, the Italian word for sauce.

By 1946, demand for their product had grown to the point that they had to open a plant. The label acquired its Venetian gondolier when the Cantisano's son, Ralph, spotted a picture of one on the back wall of a restaurant in Philadelphia. When the Cantisanos owned Ragú, sales were limited to the Northeast, but this section of the country buys so much Italian food that Ragú had 20 percent of the national supermarket spaghetti sauce market. When Chesebrough-Pond purchased Ragú from Ralph Cantisano for $43.8 million in 1969, Ragú had $22 million in annual sales.

Chesebrough-Pond predicted that spaghetti sauce would go from being an ethnic delicacy to an all-American food. In fact, today spaghetti sauce is a $550 million business, with Ragú accounting for about 60 percent of all sales. To become this successful across the country, Ragú has had to offer many sauces in addition to the Cantisanos' original recipe, Old World Style. For instance, Southerners like Ragú's spicy Thick and Hearty line, while Californians prefer the fresher, lighter taste of Ragú Fino Italian. Although Ragú tries to please different palates with different sauces, most people still doctor the sauce with their own herbs, spices, vegetables or meat once they get it in a pan. "From an emotional point of view, the minute they add to the sauce it becomes their own, something they have specially prepared for their family," Ragú president Art Gonis explains.

As for Giovanni Cantisano's son Ralph: Upon selling Ragú to Chesebrough-Pond, he signed a contract saying he wouldn't get involved in the ready-made spaghetti sauce business for three years. Three years to the day, he began Cantisano Foods, a new spaghetti sauce company just down the road from the Ragú plant and about 1,000 feet from the house at 36 Avery Street where he used to help his parents pack their sauce in mason jars.

BORDEN EAGLE BRAND SWEETENED CONDENSED MILK: THE SWEET TASTE OF SUCCESS

Before he even started the food company that made him famous, Gail Borden had already lived the lives of five average men. As a surveyor and one of the early settlers of Texas, he prepared the first typographical map of that state. As founder and editor of Texas's first permanent newspaper, he wrote a headline that became a rallying cry of the new republic: "Remember the Alamo!" He also worked as a schoolteacher, real estate salesman and customs collector. But none of these professions seemed to interest Borden as much as his avocation: inventing. He had run through quite a few inventions before hitting upon the one that made him famous.

After his wife died of yellow fever, for instance, Borden decided people should spend the hot summer months when the disease was most apt to spread in a giant refrigerated building. Borden even built a prototype building, but no one would agree to live in it.

He was forever trying to extend the life of foods by dehydrating and condensing them and once held a dinner party consisting entirely of the fruits of these experiments. Although Borden ate heartily, his friends poked at their plates and refused second helpings. After dinner, Borden brought his guests down to the beach for a ride in another of Borden's inventions: a land sailor that had no brakes. Rattled by his passengers' screams as the vehicle took on speed, Borden swung the rudder the wrong way and the vessel threw the whole group into the water. "Where's Gail?" one of the guests asked as they all scrambled out of the water. "Drowned, I do sincerely hope," another said.

Undeterred by such negativism, Borden began commercial production of a condensed meat biscuit using the anti-yellow-fever refrigerated building as his food plant. Although travelers were less than enthused by its taste (New York Central Park architect Frederick Law Olmsted threw them to the birds halfway through one of his expeditions), they nevertheless won high honors at London's Crystal Palace Exhibition in 1851. Borden got the idea for his next invention on the ship journey back from receiving that award. It seems that the two cows who were on board the ship to provide milk for children had become sick, and one infant died from drinking their contaminated milk. The cries of the other hungry babies on board inspired him to try to preserve milk as he had preserved meat, by condensing it.

Borden's first experiments produced milk with a burnt taste, but he solved that problem while visiting some Shaker friends who made maple syrup, by borrowing the idea of using a vacuum pan. Once he had evaporated the water from the milk, he added sugar as a preservative.

Although sweetened condensed milk is today considered a mere cooking ingredient, when it was invented, there was no pasteurization and it was considered nothing less than a way to save lives that were being lost to contaminated fresh milk.

Despite this, it took three years of haggling for Borden to finally be granted a patent for his process and another year to fail in his first attempt to open a milk factory before he met a New York businessman with the resources to properly back his venture. Although Borden was then 56 years old, the years of struggle made him look 70, Joe Frantz wrote in his 1951 biography of Borden. Some years after, the Civil War brought Borden huge government orders for condensed milk, thus assuring his company's success.

While Borden was still running his business, he bought a grave site at Woodlawn Cemetery in the Bronx and put a large stone monument in the shape of a milk can on it that he could see everyday on his way to work. When he died in 1874, though, his family replaced the milk can with a more conventional tombstone bearing the inscription: "I tried and failed, I tried again and again and succeeded." Borden's success inspired so many competitors—one even used the Borden name—that he was compelled to adopt the additional tradename Eagle Brand.

Borden's spokesanimal Elsie first appeared as a cartoon character in 1936 medical journal ads designed to sell doctors on condensed milk. Not long after she was introduced to ads in general interest magazines, the Borden Company set up a booth at the 1939 New York World's Fair featuring an automatic milking machine and a herd of cows. When fair visitors began asking which of the cows was Elsie, Borden executives promptly placed one of the cows in the starring role. After the fair, Elsie traveled the country, collecting keys to more than 170 cities, earning honorary college degrees and in 1946, even hosting a television show that featured a segment with chef James Beard. (A life-size Elsie puppet, not the actual cow, actually did the introduction.) In 1957, in honor of Borden's 100th anniversary, the company sponsored a "name Elsie's twin calves" contest that drew three million entries. (A grandmother from Anaheim who suggested Latabee and Lobelia won $25,000.)

Elsie still makes annual appearances at the supermarket industry's Food Marketing Institute convention in Chicago as well as at children's hospitals and festivals such as Mardi Gras. Although the Borden family of products has now expanded to include Wise potato chips, Elmer's glue, Borden ice cream and Cracker Jack, the product that started it all is still a baking staple, especially for people who make fudge.

CAMPBELL'S SOUP: M'M, M'M GOOD

Campbell's Soup, by virtue of its age and familiarity, is one of only a handful of American food products that stands as an icon of American commerce and culture. That's why, in 1962, Andy Warhol painted a Campbell's Soup can. That—plus convenience and taste—also explains why Americans buy 65 cans of Campbell's Soup every second of every day of the year and 100 cans every second in the cold winter month of January.

Americans' favorite Campbell's soups are (in order of preference): chicken noodle, cream of mushroom, tomato, cream of chicken and cream of broccoli. Early varieties that never made it to the modern age include mock turtle, mulligatawny, mutton broth, oxtail and printanier.

Campbell's Soup got its name from one of the two men that formed a fruit and preserving company in Camden, New Jersey, in 1869. Although Abram Anderson and Joseph Campbell made all sorts of condiments and jellies, their specialty was beefsteak tomatoes sliced and canned like pineapples. To emphasize their large size, the black-and-orange label featured a picture of two men carrying a tomato the size of a sofa. When Anderson left the business in 1876, Arthur Dorrance became Campbell's partner. One of the first and most important things Dorrance did was offer his nephew, John, a job with the company.

The summer after finishing his graduate studies in chemistry, John had spent some time working in Parisian kitchens and had been intrigued with the way the French chefs prepared and stored their soup. In 1897, the only soups available for commercial sale in America came in big cans, which were expensive to ship and took up too much space in the grocers'. But John Dorrance had an idea that soup could be condensed like Gail Borden had condensed milk some 40 years before. (When John Dorrance died in 1930, as president of Campbell's, he left the third-largest estate ever recorded in the United States and a will so precise it even specified his wife as the beneficiary of the gasoline left in his automobile tanks. But that's getting ahead of ourselves.)

As John Dorrance was whipping up the first batches of Campbell's Condensed Tomato Soup, Campbell's employee Heberton L. Williams attended a Thanksgiving football game between Cornell and the University of Pennsylvania at which the Cornell team members debuted their new uniforms of bright red and white. He remembered them when he attended a company meeting to decide on a new label for Campbell's brand-new soup. Also incorporated into the design was a medal Campbell's had won for the excellence of its products at the 1876 Centennial Exposition. In 1900 (the same year that Campbell died of a heart attack on the way to work), this was replaced by a gold medallion the soups won at the Paris Exposition. That medal depicts the angel of victory carrying a sheaf of wheat, representing food, and a wreath of laurel, the reward earned by the worker who sits on her shoulder. The building below belongs to the Exposition, many of whose buildings can still be seen along the Champs Élysées in Paris. The word soup was printed in large letters, to counter housewives' incredulousness that the cans could be so small.

The company decided to advertise in trolley cars

CAMPBELL'S KIDS

Campbell's Soups 10¢ a Can
ADD ZEST TO APPETITE

The Campbell Kids were modeled in the roly-poly likeness of artist-creator Grace Drayton Wiederseim. Meant to show mothers how robust kids who ate soup could be, they grew to be as popular with kids in the early 1900s as Teenage Mutant Ninja Turtles are with them in the early 1990's.

across the country. As part of his pitch to get that account, ad man Theodore E. Wiederseim, Jr., showed his wife's drawings of chubby-cheeked children. Grace Drayton Wiederseim modeled the pictures, which she dubbed "Roly-Polys," in her own image. Like her, the kids had round faces, turned-up noses and wide-set eyes. Campbell's executives thought that cute children's pictures would have great appeal to mothers who would be buying the soup and began running

them on the trolley car cards and in magazine ads. What they hadn't anticipated was the great hit the Campbell Kids would be with children. During the first decade of the new century, thousands of little kids began assembling Campbell Kids scrapbooks and so many college students wrote in for trolley car signs to decorate their dorm rooms that the company had to start charging for postage.

The Campbell Kids' stock has waxed and waned

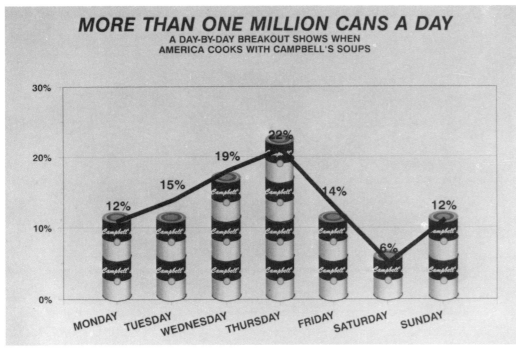

MORE THAN ONE MILLION CANS A DAY
A DAY-BY-DAY BREAKOUT SHOWS WHEN AMERICA COOKS WITH CAMPBELL'S SOUPS

Cooking with soup becomes more popular as the week wears on and peaks on Thursday, when a quarter of all recipes using soup are prepared, a Campbell's study once reported. Campbell's officials theorize this is because people are looking for something easy to make on the last hectic weekday.

most cooking with Campbell's. They found out that usage builds throughout the week, peaking on Thursday, when a quarter of all recipes using soup are prepared. (Campbell's theorizes this is because people are looking for something easy to make on the last hectic weekday.)

The most popular recipes are tuna noodle casserole, green bean bake and "glorified" baked chicken. Souperburgers and tomato soup spice cake also have their fans. But tomato soup cake almost seems normal compared to the recipe once developed to make doughnuts using tomato soup and mashed potatoes. For the adventurous, here are the ingredients.

since then. After pretty much disappearing during the Depression and World War II (when their robust appearance and happy demeanor was thought out of place), they were brought back in 1953 to sing the famous "M'm, M'm Good" song during commercial breaks of "Lassie." After a hiatus during the hip 1960s and 1970s, the Campbell Kids were revived in 1990 as a multiethnic troupe that even sang rap songs.

In 1916 the company began promoting cooking with soup. (Campbell's very first cookbook, *Helps for the Hostess*, featured tips on napkin folding and proper table etiquette as well as a section titled, "An Informal Dinner Served Without a Maid.") The effort has paid off for today one out of every three cans of Campbell's Soup and 80 percent of Campbell's Cream of Mushroom Soup are used in recipes. Campbell's once commissioned a study to find out when people did their

Tomato Soup and Mashed Potato Doughnuts

1 can tomato soup
1 cup mashed potatoes
1¼ cups sugar
5 tablespoons shortening, melted
5 cups sifted flour
5 teaspoons baking powder
1 teaspoon baking soda
3 teaspoons cinnamon
½ teaspoon nutmeg
½ teaspoon cloves

Slowly add the sugar to the soup and the potatoes. Stir in the shortening and set aside. Resift the flour with the remaining ingredients, then stir wet and dry mixtures together until well-blended. Fry in deep fat heated to 375° until golden brown. Makes 45 doughnuts.

SPAM: THE MIRACLE MEAT IN A CAN

For many years the key to one of America's most versatile cooking meats had a tiny square hole that had to be wrapped around a metal tab on the can before you began twisting it round and round. Now it's a more conventional flip top.

In either case the metal top that pops off reveals a pink brick of meat encased in a gelatinous coating: It's the home birth of a new can of SPAM® luncheon meat.

As long as there have been people who were frugal, this chopped and formed pork product has been used as a substitute for ham, bacon and other more expensive meats. The funny-sounding food appeared in a Monty Python sketch of a husband and wife dining at a restaurant where everything on the menu contains SPAM and in David Letterman's invention, SPAM-on-a-rope, for busy people who like to lunch in the shower.

There are also countless jokes from World War II GIs who ate the stuff by the frigate load. They called it "ham that didn't pass its physical" and told the story of the downed pilot who spent weeks in the jungle eating only roots and berries until he is finally found by a rescue team. But when he discovers that they have only SPAM to feed him, he runs back into the jungle. One U.S. Air Force unit stationed in the South Pacific called their island jungle Spamville. But in his biography, Nikita Khrushchev credited American shipments of SPAM with keeping his army alive.

In 1987, SPAM's 50th anniversary, the commemorative logo for the annual Cedar River Days festival in SPAM manufacturer Geo. A. Hormel & Company's hometown of Austin, Minnesota, featured a duck with a shamrock in its mouth floating in water next to a cedar tree and a giant can of SPAM luncheon meat. For the past couple of years Hormel has sponsored its own Spam Jamboree! in Austin encompassing such activities as a costume contest (children must dress up like a Spam can), a Spamburger eating contest and a bike ride to a nearby town with a population of one. SPAM was the medium for a sculpture contest held in Seattle, Washington, in 1990. First prize was captured by a replica of Stonehenge called Spamhenge. Runners-up included Uncle Spam, Spam Spade and FrankenSpam.

These are only two of many events that celebrate SPAM. In Hawaii, the state with the largest consumption of Spam per person, the Maui Mall sponsors an SPAM Cookoff where SPAM spaghetti and SPAM in a volcano were recent winners. A SPAM Olympics is held in conjunction with the Austin, Texas annual SPAM Cookoff, staged on the Sunday nearest April Fools' Day. Olympic events include speed eating and the SPAM Toss, where teams play catch with a slippery can of SPAM, stepping backward until they miss. In Pittsburgh, Pennsylvania, in April, Carnegie-Mellon University student Derek Chung holds his annual Spamfest (Offerings include SPAM pizza, Spamwiches, macaroni and SPAM, and SPAM and eggs.) "Spam partially fills you up and partially you just don't want to eat much of it," Chung explains.

But if SPAM is much maligned, it is of the good-natured kidding kind. For even after all these years, SPAM remains the most popular canned meat on America's supermarket shelves.

The SPAM story began with several thousand pounds of pork shoulder in Hormel's meat-packing plant that no one knew what to do with. In 1927, one executive got the bright idea of chopping the pork shoulder up, adding in some ham and spices and canning it in a clear gelatin casing so it would keep almost indefinitely. Hormel Spiced Ham, as it was then called, was quickly imitated by other meat packers. Responding just as quickly to the threat, Hormel offered a $100 prize to anyone who could come up with a name

◄ The "Cold or hot, SPAM® hits the spot" advertising campaign was designed to spotlight the meat's desirability around the clock. It apparently worked, for today 25 percent of all SPAM is eaten for breakfast.

▼ Although the frequency with which SPAM showed up at mess during World War II made it the butt of many jokes, it was the returning GIs who made SPAM a bestseller.

that would make their product stand out. The brother of a Hormel executive won with his suggestion of SPAM, derived by taking the "Sp" from spiced and "am" from ham.

The beginning of national distribution of SPAM was accompanied by what is believed to have been the first singing commercial. (Set to the tune of "My Bonnie Lies Over the Ocean," the lyrics went: "Spam, Spam, Spam, SPAM/Hormel's new miracle meat in a can/Tastes fine, saves time/If you want something

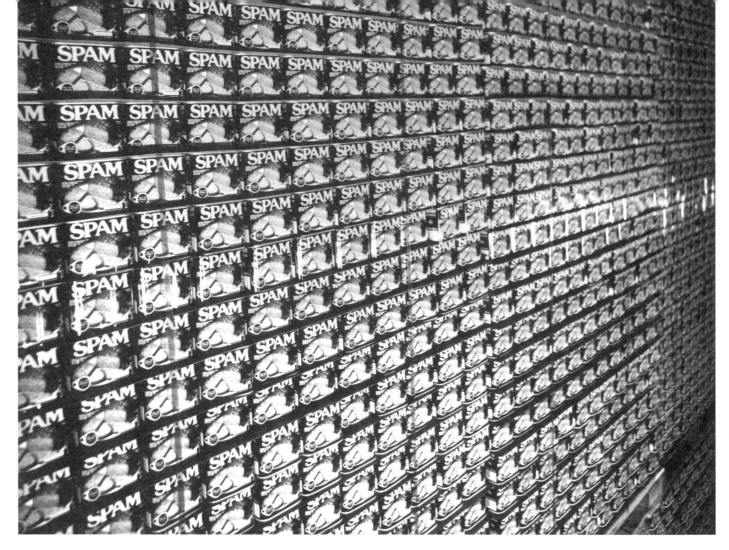

More than four billion cans of SPAM have been produced since its introduction in 1937. Americans consume 3.8 cans of SPAM every second, or 122 million cans a year.

grand, ask for SPAM.") But it was the returning GIs who made the meat a bestseller. Despite the jokes, it was apparently a taste they couldn't shake.

SPAM still holds a 75 percent share of the canned meat market in America and is served in nearly 30 percent of all American households, including that of Senator Robert Byrd of West Virginia, who reportedly eats a SPAM sandwich with mayonnaise on white bread three times a week. Country western singer

T. Graham Brown's stage costume usually includes an old SPAM key on a chain.

But nowhere is SPAM more prized than in South Korea, where black market SPAM regularly flows from U.S. military bases and locally produced knockoffs, such as Lospam, abound. In fact, young Korean men are just as likely to show up at the house of a woman they are courting with a nine-can gift pack of SPAM as wine or chocolate.

CHUN KING: FIRST CONQUEST OF A SUPERMARKET KING

Can an Italian-American find success making Chinese food in a Scandinavian section of Duluth, Minnesota? Ah so, for within nine years of when Jeno Paulucci founded Chun King in 1947, he was the largest producer of Oriental-American foods in the country.

What's even more amazing is that Chun King is only one of two popular supermarket food brands that Paulucci founded. The other bears his name, Jeno's Pizza.

Jeno Paulucci showed his talent for selling early on. The son of a poor miner, Paulucci became a fruit barker at 14 and was so good at it that when ammonia fumes badly browned 18 crates of his bananas he sold them all, at a premium price, as "exotic Argentine imports." Paulucci's penetrating hawking voice was reportedly the reason his hometown passed an ordinance forbidding street vending.

Paulucci's first job out of school was as a salesman for a wholesale grocery firm. When he began earning more in commissions than the president of the company earned in salary, he was told that he too was going to be put on salary. So he quit and started a business selling dehydrated garlic. But after realizing the limitations of that market ("How much garlic could anybody use? A little bit goes a long way," he reasoned), he borrowed $2,500 to rent a Quonset hut where he could grow and can bean sprouts, that most inexpensive of Oriental cooking ingredients. He named his new firm after Chungking, the wartime capital of China then much in the news. He split the name and dropped a *g* to avoid trademark problems.

Hired to entertain at a community festival in Duluth, MN in 1947, comedian Bob Hope donned the Duke of Duluth's crown and cape and posed in the booth of a brand-new Chun King Chinese-American food company as a goof to the delight of company founder Jeno Paulucci (left).

Soon his line of foods expanded to chop suey and chow mein. To keep costs down, Paulucci went to Florida to check on the source of his celery supply. Watching a farmer cutting the celery into bunches, he realized how many of the outside stalks were being wasted. "So I brought my own truck and asked the farmer if I could take the leftover celery at $10 a ton," Paulucci recalled. Paulucci ended up paying

$20, but it was still about four to five times less than what his competitors were paying. Paulucci decided to spend the savings on the advertising that was to make Chun King a household name. One of the most memorable ads claimed that nine out of ten doctors recommended Chun King. As an off-screen voice loudly protested this, the camera panned down a row of ten doctors in white coats, all but one of whom were Chinese.

But much of the company's success can be credited to Paulucci's willingness to do whatever needed to be done. According to *Business Week* magazine, when Paulucci was threatened with losing one of his first big customers, the Food Fair supermarket chain, he flew to Philadelphia to conduct a quality test with the company's chief buyer. Opening a can of chop suey, Paulucci found himself staring down at a huge grasshopper. Without blinking an eye or letting the buyer see, Paulucci choked down the grasshopper and saved the account.

In 1967, Paulucci sold Chun King to R. J. Reynolds Industries, Inc., for $63 million, distributing $2 million of it to employees as a parting gift. He started Jeno's a year later and sold it to Pillsbury for $150 million in 1985.

After a string of unsuccessful restaurant and real estate ventures, Paulucci is back in Duluth making a new line of frozen Italian dinners named after his mother, Michelina. Judging from his past successes, Budget Gourmet and Stouffer's had better watch out.

OCEAN SPRAY: A BERRY FINE JELLIED SAUCE

Its unadulterated flavor could, in the words of one writer, "raise blisters on asbestos." The fact that cranberries rank second (only behind lemons) on the U.S. Agriculture Department's list of crops with the largest gross return therefore seems wholly unexpected and is largely due to the ingenuity of a growers' cooperative known as Ocean Spray.

Cranberries are one of three native American fruits (Concord grapes and blueberries are the other two) and in fact, it was native Americans who introduced cranberries to the Pilgrims about when they landed here in the 1600s. The Pilgrims named them crane berries (later shortened to cranberries) because the pink cranberry blossoms reminded them of the heads of cranes.

Commercial cultivation of cranberries began in about 1817 and spread so rapidly that by 1912, large portions of the crop of 512,000 barrels rotted for want of a market. To help save his business, Cape Cod Cranberry Company president Marcus L. Urann began whipping up batches of cranberry sauce and canning them for year-round sale. Because salt spray drifted over his company's Cape Cod cranberry bogs, he called the product Ocean Spray Cape Cod Cranberry Sauce.

By the end of World War I, several other cranberry growers were also making cranberry sauce. Rather than compete with one another, they merged with Urann's company in 1930 to form the Ocean Spray growers' cooperative (which now numbers 700 members, or 80 percent of all American cranberry growers). That same year Ocean Spray Cranberry Juice Cocktail was introduced as "a pleasant, smooth drink with delicious flavor and sure relief from faintness, exhaustion, and thirst. A glass when retiring promotes sleep and a clean mouth in the morning—even to the smoker."

The cooperative didn't start selling fresh bagged berries until 1946. From 1946 to 1959, the bulk of sales was of sauces and fresh berries during the fall holiday season.

In November of 1959 a government announcement that a herbicide used by some cranberry growers had caused cancer in laboratory rats cast the whole future of the cranberry industry in doubt. For several years hardly anybody served cranberry sauce at the Thanksgiving table. As farmers struggled through the scare, Ocean Spray management decided they were going to have to monitor crop-growing practices more carefully, broaden their offerings beyond one or two cranberry products and begin to create rather than simply satisfy demand for cranberry products.

First they moved aggressively into the juice business, sweetening their cranberry juice cocktail more to people's liking and introducing such popular juice blends as Cranapple, Cran Grape and Cran Raspberry. In 1981, Ocean Spray became the first American company to put drinks in aseptic containers. Despite some missteps (most notably Cranprune), juices now account for two thirds of all company business.

Today Ocean Spray's museum and visitor's center, Cranberry World, Water Street, Plymouth, MA 02360 (508-747-2350), is just down the street from where the Pilgrims probably first ate the fruit. There, from May through November, tourists can examine a display of old cranberry boxes, try samples of the company's latest drinks and observe the test of a really good cranberry (namely, whether it can bounce over an assembly line barrier four inches high).

RICE AND PASTA

WILL THE REAL UNCLE BEN PLEASE STAND UP?

Uncle Ben was a black rice farmer renowned throughout Houston, Texas, for the quality of rice he delivered to local millers. The details of his life story have been lost to history, but in the 1940s, when a Texan named Gordon Harwell was looking for a brand name under which to sell converted rice, Uncle Ben came readily to mind.

The procedure for converting rice was developed by a British scientist, but Harwell was the first to bring it to the United States. In conversion, the rice is steamed under pressure to drive the vitamins and minerals from

Uncle Ben's rice products are named after a legendary black rice farmer, but the man who ended up on the package was Chicago restaurant maitre d' Frank Brown. Pictured is one of the very first Uncle Ben's packages.

the outer bran layer, which is later discarded, into the center of the grain, which remains. In addition to being more nutritious, converted rice lasts longer than regular rice and is less vulnerable to infestation—all things that made it highly attractive to the U.S. military, then in the midst of fighting World World II. So Harwell had no trouble getting government permission to build his first plant, and from 1943 to 1946 all the rice he made went into mess kits.

After the war ended, Harwell and his business partner met in a Chicago restaurant to make plans to market converted rice to the general public. During that dinner, they settled on the name Uncle Ben's. Since the real Uncle Ben was already long dead, they asked the restaurant's black maître d', Frank Brown, to pose for the picture still on the rice packages. That's why the product might better be called Uncle Frank's instead of Uncle Ben's.

MINUTE RICE: MARKETING BE NIMBLE, RICE BE QUICK

If a man identifying himself as a cousin of the king of Afghanistan and carrying a package big enough to contain a hot plate tried to walk into General Foods headquarters today, he'd probably find security officers escorting him to the nearest exit within a few seconds. People were more trusting in 1941. That's when Ataullah K. Ozai Durrani walked into a General Foods executive's office, whipped out a hot plate and cooked up a pot of rice in only 10 minutes.

Knowing that a lot of housewives found rice making difficult and tedious, the executive set Durrani up in a General Foods lab to prepare more samples of precooked rice. Soon the company set its own people to work on using Durrani's idea to precook, then quick dry large quantities of rice in a way that did not require huge amounts of heat or result in great loss or spoilage. They had only been working on the problem a year when World War II broke out, and the govern-

ment commandeered Minute Rice test production facilities for use in creating an "instant" rice for C-ration packages. So American GIs served as guinea pigs in Minute Rice's development. Among the things GF scientists learned during the war years:

- To prevent the rice from shrinking, it was better to cook it only partially rather than fully;

- The best way to tell if the rice was cooked fully enough was to count the number of holes in each grain under a microscope;

- Long-grain rice was better suited to precooking than short or medium.

To help acceptance of the product when it was first introduced into grocery stores in 1949, Minute Rice was put in almost the same red, white and blue checkerboard package as the already established Minute Tapioca. (Minute Tapioca had been invented by a Massachusetts woman when her boarder complained that her tapioca was too lumpy and ought to be put through a coffee grinder. The tapioca is also partially precooked for faster preparation.)

Minute Rice's popularity was also hastened by the first consumer advertising ever done for a rice. It included newspaper ads with mock banner headlines screaming, "Rice Was Never Like This Before—So Easy, So Quick, So Sure-to-Be-Wonderful." Within

General Foods, Minute Rice was promoted through a sales event that featured an appearance by the International Rice Queen and articles in the company newsletter. In one such article, the Minute Way of cooking rice, "standardized, quick, surefire," and requiring only three photo frames to explain, was contrasted to "When Mrs. Consumer Starts from Scratch," which takes six steps and includes a lot of washing and doubt. In step 4 a housewife is shown draining the rice after cooking, but, the copy explains, this "is usually followed by another washing." Step 5 is "testing the cooking—and deciding to leave it on longer. After 40 minutes, ordinary rice "should be done," but, the copy asks, "How light and fluffy?"

Thanks to all this, initial sales of Minute Rice were strong—but fell off afterward because, General Foods market researchers discovered, housewives used potatoes a lot more often. The General Foods consumer kitchens were set to work to correct that by making recipes for Minute Rice. These were featured in ads that exclaimed "Quick, quick fixin'! Grand feastin'! Amazing new rice discovery makes marvelous hustle-up meals." Just so there were no misunderstandings, each recipe specified preparation time and when it should be served: "Sunday night snack, 15 minutes"; "Dinner De Luxe, 30 minutes"; "Hearty man-size meal, 15 minutes."

Recipes continue to play an important role in the sales of Original Minute Rice and Minute Premium, a new quick-cooking rice introduced in 1988 using a different type of long-grained rice. A year later, General Foods introduced Minute Instant Brown Rice for those people who wanted to eat healthy in only a few minutes.

RICE-A-RONI: THE SAN FRANCISCO TREAT

Rice-A-Roni holds the distinction of being one of the only food products with a city as its advertising spokesman. Since 1961, the sight of a cable car lumbering up a hill with its bell clanging has become synonymous with the seasoned rice and pasta dish.

The founder of Rice-A-Roni, Domenico de Domenico, actually came from Italy. The food company he founded in San Francisco in 1912 specialized in spaghetti and pasta products. Rice-A-Roni began as a recipe de Domenico printed on the side of one of the pasta packages. In 1958, the recipe became a product sold in area grocery stores; in 1961, it began to be distributed nationally as well.

By then the dish had become such a local specialty—and San Francisco had such a reputation for fine food—that it seemed natural to make San Francisco and its charming cable cars the focus of the first national advertising campaign. The "San Francisco Treat" jingle was written to the inversed melody of "Barney Google," a popular song from the 1920s.

In the 1980s, however, San Francisco became known mainly as a center for earthquakes and the AIDS epidemic. Although a tiny cable car still appeared on the package, new Rice-A-Roni owner Quaker Oats dropped San Francisco as the theme of the product's ads in 1987.

But consumers' hearts were apparently still in San Francisco. For by 1991, Rice-A-Roni's ad campaign was back along the blue and windy sea.

KRAFT MACARONI & CHEESE DINNER: A DEAL OF A MEAL

It's cheap, can sit on the shelf until whenever you need it and is quick, easy and even fun to make. Who is immune to that special thrill when you pour the packet of dry cheese into the pan and the cooked noodles suddenly glisten with color? Is it any wonder, then, that Kraft Macaroni & Cheese Dinner is the most popular packaged dinner and one of the top six best-selling of all dry goods sold in the supermarket?

Kraft Dinner was inspired by a St. Louis salesman who convinced grocers to stock a packaged dinner he had created by tying Kraft grated American cheese to Tenderoni Macaroni. He was trying to push the macaroni, but when Kraft got wind of what he was doing, they hired the salesman to promote the product for them, introducing it nationally in 1937. The very first Kraft Dinners were packaged in yellow boxes, but that was soon changed to blue, prompting Kraft employees to call it "Blue Box," an insiders' nickname still in use today.

Kraft Dinner was first advertised on the Kraft Music Hall radio show as "A meal for four in nine minutes for an everyday price of 19 cents." But it was frequently on sale for as little as half that price. Today it costs about 49 cents and takes only seven minutes to make.

Although Kraft Dinner was popular from the first year (when 8 million boxes were sold), World War II turned it into a phenomenon. Because Kraft Macaroni & Cheese was a substitute for the fresh meat and dairy products being rationed during World War II, two boxes required only one rationing coupon, and in 1943 careful shoppers bought 80 million boxes.

Kraft Dinner also fit in with the new demand for convenience products after the war. Advertisements for the dinner at this time told busy housewives not to "hurry, puff and wheeze. There's a main dish that's a breeze."

Around this time, Kraft Dinner was responsible for one of the company's most successful premium promotions ever. After discovering that one box of cooked Kraft Dinner fit perfectly into a 6½-inch Mirro aluminum ring mold, Kraft began offering the molds as a premium for box tops and 25 cents. In one year Kraft sold more Mirro molds than had been sold in the history of the Mirro Company.

Today Kraft sells about 300 million boxes of Blue Box every year. Sales peak during Lent, when Christians who are prohibited from eating meat turn to Kraft Dinner as an alternative. In addition to the original Blue Box, Kraft now also sells dinners with macaroni in the shape of teddy bears, dinosaurs and wheels (of special appeal to children) and a deluxe version that contains a pouch of yellow cheese sauce in place of the powder.

Once when food writers Jane and Michael Stern heard that Kraft was going to drop Blue Box in favor of the deluxe version, they bought every Blue Box in their town's supermarkets and stored them in their basement. Fortunately the rumor was false.

Last I heard, the Sterns were still eating their way through their hoard.

HAMBURGER HELPER: HELPING MAKE ENDS MEAT

Hamburger Helper was invented in 1970, in the midst of a meat shortage. Even an inexpensive meat like hamburger was taking a bite out of families' food budgets, and so General Mills invented Helper as a way of helping housewives to stretch a pound of hamburger into a satisfying meal for a family of five. A companion product for use with the equally lowly can of tuna was introduced within two years.

Once the meat shortage was over, the Helper concept changed to trying to render cookbooks obsolete. The Helper box of seasoning or sauce and rice or pasta packets, along with some canned tuna or fresh hamburger or chicken (after Chicken Helper made its national debut in 1984) seemed to be able to reproduce virtually any popular dish or flavor.

Want a potpie? Try Tuna Helper Pot Pie, complete with top and bottom crusts and cream sauce with peas and carrots. Want Sloppy Joes? Hamburger Helper Sloppy Joe Bake Dinner has a crust mix flavored like a hamburger bun. Adventurous enough for ethnic cuisine? Check out Hamburger Helper Rice Oriental Dinner mix, Hamburger Helper Pizzabake or Hamburger Helper Tacobake dinner. Feeling homesick for the dishes Mom used to make? How about Skillet Chicken Helper Creamy Mushroom with Noodles, Tuna Helper Tetrazzini or the quintessential (and best-selling) Hamburger Helper Cheeseburger Macaroni?

Although the Helpers are now only designed to accompany hamburger, tuna and chicken, the company seems open to expanding them to more. Referring to a cartoon that shows a supermarket featuring pork brains and next to it a box of "Pork Brains Helper," a company spokesman said, "If ostrich meat were in vogue with ordinary American shoppers, you can bet we would have Ostrich Meat Helper."

Like Spam, Twinkies and Wonder Bread, Hamburger Helper has come in for a fair share of ribbing. Chevy Chase did some tweaking of it in a dinner scene from the movie *National Lampoon's Vacation* where his hopelessly cheap inlaws serve a meal that they affectionately describe as "Hamburger Helper without the hamburger." In what looked like an effort to placate the crowd of gourmets growing in America in the 1970s, General Mills came out with a Tuna Helper Macaroni Newburg main dish mix, which boasted of containing "a hint of wine" in 1973. (It was discontinued because of poor sales in 1978.) General Mills has yet to make "Top Sirloin Helper." Spotting this product was enough to make a shopper in one recent cartoon realize, "This must be a gourmet place."

But for every person who sees Hamburger Helper as a sign of just how far American cooking has sunk, there are perhaps five others who value the products for their economy and ease and buy them regularly. In fact, speaking in terms of dollar volume, the Helper line sells better than any other product that bears Betty Crocker's red spoon trademark—including her cake mixes.

LIPTON ONION SOUP MIX: ELIXIR OF THE MEDIOCRE CHEF

Lipton onion soup mix is the magic powder of the mediocre chef. Where Julia Child might sauté some onions and garlic in some butter and wine—knowing instinctively just how much to use and when—most people use Lipton Onion Recipe Soup Mix (or its wet cousin, Campbell's mushroom soup), all pre-measured and ready to go.

A product of Lipton, a food company started by a successful Scottish grocer who became famous for retail sales of tea in bags, onion soup mix was developed in 1952 as a convenient, easy-to-store form of soup. In December of 1954, Lipton executives noticed an inexplicably sharp rise in sales of onion soup mix in California. Eventually they traced the climb to a soup-mix-inspired dip recipe that was being passed around from housewife to housewife, subsequently showing up on the pages of a newspaper food section in that state.

The original recipe called for mixing two envelopes of soup mix to one cup of sour cream, but nutritionists in the test kitchens of Lipton thought it too strong. Nobly forgoing the temptation to leave the recipe alone and create more sales, they printed a recipe for California dip on the back of the soup mix package that advises using only one envelope of mix to one 16-ounce container of sour cream. The California dip discovery also led the company's dietitians to get busy making up more recipes, including often-requested ones for meat loaf (see below) and onion roasted potatoes.

"Lipton onion soup mix is basically a broth base with toasted onion pieces. That makes it very adaptable for recipes," notes Anna Marie Coccia, Lipton Test Kitchens manager. "Wet, it can be used in just about anything that could use a broth. Dry, it can be used as a seasoning."

Shoppers seem to agree. Nowadays, Lipton research shows that few of the people who buy Lipton Onion Recipe Soup Mix make onion soup.

"Souperior" Meat Loaf

1 envelope Lipton Onion Recipe Soup Mix
2 lbs. ground beef
1½ cups fresh breadcrumbs
2 eggs
¾ cup water
⅓ cup ketchup

Preheat oven to 350 degrees. Combine above. Shape ingredients into a loaf and place in 2 quart oblong baking pan. Bake 1 hour or until done.

BAKING PRODUCTS

GOLD MEDAL: THE FLOUR OF BELLS AND WASHBURN

People thought Cadwallader C. Washburn was crazy to build a big new flour mill in Minneapolis in 1856. Because of the hard winters there, plains farmers had to grow a hard-kerneled wheat that produced a darker flour than most consumers liked. So how could he possibly make money?

By hiring an engineer to invent a system of air currents and sieves that separated the bran, resulting in a flour every bit as white as other brands and actually superior in some baking properties, that's how.

Washburn pioneered other advances in milling as well, including becoming the first American miller to crush wheat with steel rollers—a great improvement over stone. When an explosion caused by flour dust leveled his plant in 1898, Washburn designed a machine to remove the dust from the air that is still used in flour mills today.

Partially as a result of Washburn's innovations, Minneapolis grew to become one of the nation's major milling centers. The high quality of Washburn's product was confirmed when he and business partner John Crosby entered their flours in the first Millers' International Exhibition in 1880 and swept the first three awards. Washburn and Crosby began advertising their highest grade of flour based on its Gold Medal award, stenciling it on the heads of the 196-pound barrels that stood in grocery stores of the day as flour dispensers. When, in 1905, flour began to be sold in small, consumer sizes, the barrelhead design was simply shrunk down to fit on the bags. It is the one seen on the bags today.

Succeeding Washburn as president of the Washburn

Crosby Company was the first in a line of men from the Bell family who led the company through the next 80 years. James S. Bell was known as an aggressive merchandiser. It was under his leadership that in 1921 the company ran a picture puzzle contest with a prize of a Gold Medal flour pincushion that attracted so much correspondence a fictitious character named Betty Crocker had to be created to answer it all (see *Betty Crocker*).

It was also under Bell that company advertising manager Benjamin Seth Bull created an advertising slogan that the company used in magazines, on billboards and on the bags until the late 1950s: "Eventually—Why Not Now?" It happened one day when Bull was editing a particularly wordy text detailing the attributes of Gold Medal flour. Bull slashed this word and that until, upon finishing, he found he had left nothing except for the word "Eventually." As a lesson to the copywriter, Bull scrawled in the margin, "Why not now?" But after having written this down, he thought better of it and threw it into the wastebasket. Later, the paper was retrieved by James Ford Bell, a perceptive young employee who convinced Bull to try it as a slogan. He also happened to be the son of the company president. Is it any wonder that he soon became president himself?

Despite Washburn Crosby's many successes, the varying pricing and distribution practices for flour in different states made it hard for the company to expand beyond its own market. Officials were also frustrated by their vulnerability to wheat shortages caused by local storms. Three years after becoming president of the Washburn Crosby Company in 1925, James Ford Bell engineered the solution to some of these problems by merging his company with six other millers to create General Mills. (In 1929, they were joined by the largest miller on the Pacific Coast, the Sperry Flour Company.) To celebrate the formation of the new company, recipes were packed in bags of Gold Medal flour, a practice that continues to this day.

The next Bell to take over (James's son Charles) closed down half the company's flour mills and began a diversification program that made General Mills a major producer of toys (Monopoly, Lionel Trains), costume jewelry, clothes and furniture. In the 1970s, the company began to sell off these businesses. Today General Mills's only business is food.

BETTY CROCKER: PATRON SAINT OF AMERICAN COOKING

Responsible and reliable she may be, but Betty Crocker also harbors her share of contradictions. Although she is supposed to represent domesticity, it's never been clear whether or not she's married. At 70-plus years, she has yet to show one wrinkle. Although known by 90 percent of Americans, she has never really existed.

Whatever her faults, Betty Crocker is still the patron saint of American cooking, with more than 55 million cookbooks and 130 General Mills food products (with annual sales upward of $500 million) bearing her face or name.

The legend of Betty Crocker began in 1921 when the Washburn Crosby Company of Minneapolis (the forerunner to General Mills) ran a picture puzzle in a national magazine promoting Gold Medal flour. The prize was a pincushion that resembled a Gold Medal flour sack. The Washburn Crosby Company was surprised not only by the number of people who entered the contest (more than 30,000) but also by the number of people who enclosed baking questions along with the completed puzzle.

Although men and women employees pitched in to handle the huge volume of mail, company ad man Samuel C. Gale thought the replies would have more weight if they were signed by a woman. So he made up a name: Betty because it sounded friendly and was popular at the time; Crocker to honor a company director who had just retired.

At first, Betty was only a name and a signature (a secretary named Florence Lindebergan won an in-house handwriting contest for the honor of supplying the latter), but between 1924 and 1948 she was also host of broadcasting's first cooking show, "Betty Crocker Cooking School of the Air." In the early days, each radio show was recorded by actresses with different regional accents. The audience was estimated at about a million.

Judging from the holiday presents and letters that poured into General Mills, most women believed Betty Crocker was a real person. One letter was from the wife of Ernest Hemingway, then on safari in Africa, asking how she might help the natives improve the taste of their flour. In the late 1930s the company's lawyers were becoming increasingly nervous about possible public deception. But Betty's value to the company was so great that they decided to "take the business risk of continuing the personification of Betty Crocker."

Some of the later Betty Crocker broadcasts combined cooking with advice and other features. During the war years, the U.S. State Department enlisted Betty's help in hosting "Your Nation's Rations," a radio show that featured recipes based on effective use of the then restricted food supply. Television's "Bride and Groom," first broadcast in 1952, was a more sedate precursor to "The Newlywed Game." On it, Betty interviewed newlyweds and coached brides on the preparation of their husband's favorite dishes.

While a number of different actresses portrayed Betty on radio and television, her official face was always a painting of the supposedly ideal American housewife.

Herewith, a few crumbs of trivia about the seven Betty Crocker portraits:

1936: Neysa McMein painted the first portrait, a composite of the features of a number of women who worked in the company's home service department and who therefore performed many Betty Crocker–like functions. She had pursed lips, a pointed nose, a hard stare—a formidable woman.

1955: General Mills commissioned six artists to paint portraits and picked the favorite of 1,600 women in a consumer survey. One of the losers was Norman Rockwell. This Betty looks quite friendly but also old (she has gray hair) and plain. "You don't have to look like a missionary to cook well," one woman complained in a letter to the company.

1965 and 1968: Both painted by magazine illustrator Joe Bowler, both dramatic departures from the first two portraits. Here Betty Crocker looked much more modern—some thought a lot like consumer activist Betty Furness.

1972: This Betty Crocker looked stiff in a 1970s hairstyle and clothes, and quickly dated. The company said she looked more businesslike, but the National Organization for Women apparently disagreed, for shortly after her unveiling it filed a class action suit charging General Mills with sex discrimination for perpetuating the image of Crocker as a homemaker.

1980: Although the NOW suit was thrown out of court, General Mills must have gotten the message because this Betty is all business. The face was identical to the 1965 Betty, but with a shorter haircut and frosted highlights to make her look more mature. But some said she looked too old, formal and unapproachable.

1986: The latest portrait has been called a cross between actress Mariette Hartley and TV personality Kathleen Sullivan. New York artist Harriet Pertichik shortened Betty's formerly long, patrician nose and gave her a sturdier jaw. She is the first Betty Crocker who looks as though she could dominate on a racquetball court as well as in the workplace or in a battle to get her kids off to school in the morning.

But all seven portraits shared some features, showing a serious, conservative and well-organized person with brown hair, blue eyes and a red shirt or suit with white at the neck.

In the mid-1970s, during the move toward sleeker, more high-tech packaging, Betty Crocker's picture was taken off all packages of General Mills food, including her own cake and brownie mixes, and replaced by Betty Crocker's red spoon trademark. Today her face appears only on the best-selling *Betty Crocker Cookbook*, now in its 40th edition.

If it seems Betty Crocker is reverting to her original, more limited role as purveyor of recipes and ambassador of corporate goodwill, it could be because of what Mercedes Bates, former director of the Betty Crocker Food and Nutrition Center in Minneapolis, once said: "Today it would be impossible to create Betty Crocker. Consumers are just too sophisticated."

PILLSBURY'S WHITE THUMB CONTEST

The Pillsbury Bake-Off event is to housewives what the Miss America contest used to be to teenage girls. Even today, when more than half of American wives work outside the home, the Bake-Off with its $135,000 in total cash prizes (the top prize is $50,000 and new kitchen appliances) makes the Bake-Off contest the Olympics of amateur chefs.

In fact, the very first Bake-Off contest, held in New York City in 1949, or right after women returned to their kitchens after working in factories during World War II, was actually called the Grand National Recipe and Baking Contest. Then as now the goal of the contest was to get America cooking with Pillsbury products—although for the first 18 years, the only eligible product was Pillsbury Best flour. Pillsbury Best was the product company founder Charles Pillsbury started making when he took controlling interest in a Minneapolis mill in 1869. (One interesting footnote: The

great-grandson of Pillsbury, also named Charles, roomed with cartoonist Garry Trudeau at Yale and served as the model for the lead character in Trudeau's Pulitzer Prize-winning newspaper strip, "Doonesbury.") Now Bake-Off recipes can also use all sorts of Pillsbury mixes as well as Green Giant frozen and canned vegetables.

There is perhaps no better measure of cooking trends in America than the recipes that are submitted to the Pillsbury Bake-Off event every year. What follows is a decade-by-decade description of those contests and their entries.

The 1950s: The complexity of recipes reflected the many hours women spent in the kitchen trying to live up to the image of womanhood displayed on such popular TV shows as "Ozzie and Harriet" and "Father Knows Best." The healthy postwar economy was reflected in rich, gourmet-type main meals and the prevalence of desserts (which captured eight out of 10 of the grand prizes this decade). Even as Pillsbury and other companies introduced cake mixes into the marketplace, scratch cakes represented the largest

For years, General Electric supplied stoves for the Bake-Off. In 1961, GE spokesman Ronald Reagan appeared at the 13th contest, here with contestant Mrs. W. G. Baldwin, Jr. of Pittsboro, MI.

category of Bake-Off entries. Favorite Bake-Off recipes from this decade include Orange Kiss-Me Cake (a loaf cake topped with orange juice and nuts), Snappy Turtle Cookies (brown sugar cookies with a chocolate shell) and Peanut Blossoms (peanut butter cookies topped with Hershey's Kisses).

The 1960s: In recognition of women's growing involvement in activities outside the home, the theme of Pillsbury's 1966 Bake-Off contest was the Busy Lady. Recipes for one-step cakes, press-in-the-pan pie crusts, bar cookies and casseroles as well as those using cake mixes and ready-to-spread frostings began to dominate. The second-prize winner in the 1966 contest, Tunnel of Fudge Cake, used only six ingredients, including frosting mix, and created a run on sales for a type of pan then unfamiliar to most American cooks. In 1968, for the first time, there were new categories for recipes using Pillsbury cake and hot roll mixes and refrigerated dough. A refrigerated dough recipe, Magic Marshmallow Crescent Puffs, captured the top prize in 1969. It was one of many submissions that year with a name that referred to the moon landing (more intentional references included Cheesy Moon Bread, Space Age Onion Ring, Moon Craters and Astro-Nut).

The 1970s: America's increased interest in health was reflected in heartier and more homespun recipes for soups, stews, cobblers, dumplings and shortcakes—many of which employed such "natural" ingredients as whole grain flours and cereals, fruits and vegetables, honey, maple syrup and nuts and seeds. In 1970 and 1971, special awards for most nutritious recipe were chosen by computer.

The 1980s and Beyond: Ethnic recipes have become popular. Interest in convenience remains, with cake and brownie mixes being used like flour was in the early days. Other trends have included a revival in pie recipes due to Pillsbury's new All Ready refrigerator pie crust and the introduction of a microwave category in 1984. In 1990, oat bran showed up in huge amounts in all types of foods. Health concerns were also reflected in the more than two-thirds of recipes that contained no salt (in 1949, nearly all recipes had it). At the same time, baby boomers weaned on peanut butter began using it to make all types of fancy desserts.

These days the Pillsbury Bake-Off event is held every even-numbered year. Entry forms are usually available in the spring preceding. The deadline for entries is in October, and the 100 finalists are notified in mid-December, sometimes with some difficulty. Pillsbury officials once had to employ the help of forest rangers, the state police and park officials to notify one contestant who was on an extended camping trip.

All finalists win expense-paid trips to the Bake-Off site (usually in some warm vacation spot) plus supplies and equipment to prepare two versions of their recipes.

Magic Marshmallow Crescent Puffs

¼ cup sugar
2 tablespoons flour
1 teaspoon cinnamon
2 (8-oz.) cans Pillsbury refrigerated Quick Crescent dinner rolls
16 large marshmallows
¼ cup margarine or butter, melted

Glaze
½ cup powdered sugar
½ teaspoon vanilla
2 to 3 teaspoons milk
¼ cup chopped nuts, if desired

Heat oven to 375 degrees. In small bowl, combine sugar, flour and cinnamon. Separate dough into 16 triangles. Dip 1 marshmallow in margarine; roll in sugar mixture. Place marshmallow on wide end of triangle. Roll up starting at wide end of triangle to opposite point. Completely cover marshmallow with dough; firmly pinch edges to seal. Dip 1 end in remaining margarine; place, margarine side down, in ungreased large muffin cup or 6-oz. custard cup. Repeat with remaining marshmallows. Bake at 375 degrees for 12 to 15 minutes or until golden brown. (Place foil or cookie sheet on rack below muffin cups to guard against spillage.) Immediately remove from muffin cups; cool on wire racks.

In small bowl, blend powdered sugar, vanilla and enough milk for desired drizzling consistency. Drizzle over warm rolls. Sprinkle with nuts. Makes 16 rolls.

According to one journalist who covered the event, about half of all 100 finalists bring some kind of lucky equipment with them. One brought a carpenter's level to make sure the oven was level before she put her cake in. Contestants have varying reactions to the stresses of the Bake-Off atmosphere—from the woman who was cool enough to dance a hula for photographers while her creation was baking to the one who became so flustered that she forgot that she had placed her pie on a chair beside the oven to cool—and absent-mindedly sat on it!

Included above is the grand prize winner in the twentieth Bake-off contest in 1969, as well as an enduringly popular recipe.

BISQUICK: AMERICA'S FIRST BAKING MIX

Ablack chef with the Southern Pacific Railroad had the idea that inspired America's first baking mix, Bisquick, and by extension all the cake, muffin and pancake mixes that now line supermarket grocery aisles.

Carl Smith, a salesman for General Mills's new Western regional division (the recently acquired Sperry Flour Company), had boarded a train to San Francisco late one night in 1930. He hadn't eaten dinner. Although he didn't hold out much hope of getting a hot meal, he went to the dining car anyway. To his surprise, the dinner he was served was both hot and delicious and included freshly made biscuits.

After dinner, Smith went to the galley to compliment the chef, whose identity has been lost, and to ask him how he had been able to produce the biscuits so quickly. The man explained that he had made a practice of keeping a blended mixture of lard, flour, baking powder and salt in the icebox so that when a late order came in, he could make biscuits without measuring, mixing or sifting. Being in the baking business, Smith began to wonder if there were commercial possibilities in the chef's idea.

The next day Smith talked about the idea with the company's head chemist, Charles Kress. Kress could foresee a problem keeping the shortening in such a product from going rancid. But he had an idea of how to solve the problem: use sesame oil, a substance Kress knew would keep its sweetness even in combination with flour. It was the oil Bisquick first used. To protect this information from General Mills's competitors, sesame oil was for many years only referred to as Ingredient s. (In recent years, it has been replaced by soybean and/or cottonseed oils.)

It was assumed the new product would be sold only in the West, where Smith worked. But upon hearing of the product, General Mills president Donald Davis insisted that it go national right away. Davis also gave the product its name—"Bis" for biscuit and "quick" for how quickly it could be made.

Advertising for Bisquick promised it would allow even the most inexperienced bride or incompetent housewife to make perfect biscuits with less than 90 seconds preparation. "Happy Husbands Cheer for Wives as Old-Time Hot Biscuits Come Back!" read the headline of an ad that also featured this bit of mealtime dialogue between one husband and wife.

> HUSBAND: "Honey, you're a wow! These are the real old-time hot biscuits!"
>
> WIFE: "Only one difference, dear. They're so much fluffier, lighter and easy to digest.... Due to that new-type vegetable shortening and the way it is mixed in Bisquick."

Within seven months, such women had purchased more than half a million cases of Bisquick. Within a year, 95 imitators appeared on the grocery shelves beside it. But Bisquick had such name recognition and such a head start that by 1933, all but six competitors had disappeared.

Before long, consumers and home economists at General Mills had discovered dozens of uses for Bisquick. The company detailed some of them in the booklets "101 Delicious Bisquick Creations" (1933) and the provocatively titled "How to Take a Trick a Day" (1935). In the latter, the housewife reader followed General Mills spokeswoman Betty Crocker around the country as she obtained Bisquick recipes from society ladies and starlets such as Bette Davis (who told of eating ham biscuits in her dressing room made with Bisquick).

The company continues to produce Bisquick recipe booklets for Bisquick and now also for the new Bisquick Reduced Fat, but if you don't have one handy, the Bisquick box is plastered with popular recipes such as Impossible Pie—in which Bisquick batter is poured over or combined with hamburger and cheese, pumpkin, cherry, taco or seafood fillings only to fall, during baking, to the bottom and form a magical pielike crust.

A recent box of Bisquick boasts that more people make pancakes with Bisquick than any single brand of pancake mix. When one considers all this, Bisquick might today more accurately be called "Bakquick."

Impossible Cheeseburger Pie

1 pound ground beef
1½ cups chopped onion
½ teaspoon salt
¼ teaspoon pepper
1½ cups milk
¾ cup Bisquick baking mix
3 eggs
2 tomatoes, sliced
1 cup shredded cheddar or process American cheese (4 oz.)

Heat oven to 400 degrees. Grease pie plate, 10 by 1½ inches, or square baking dish, 8 × 8 × 2 inches, or six 10-oz. custard cups. Cook and stir ground beef and onion in 10-inch skillet over medium heat until brown; drain. Stir in salt and pepper. Spread in plate. Beat milk, baking mix and eggs 15 seconds in blender on high, 1 minute with wire whisk or with hand beater until smooth. Pour into plate. Bake 30 to 35 minutes. Top with tomatoes; sprinkle with cheese. Bake 5 to 8 minutes longer or until knife inserted in center comes out clean. Cool 5 minutes before serving. Makes 6 to 8 servings. (Recipe used with the permission of General Mills, Inc.)

RECOMMENDED BY DUNCAN HINES

Based on what you've read so far, you're probably thinking Duncan Hines was a guy who started a small bakery that became popular locally for its delicious cakes and grew into a large cake mix operation that eventually was taken over by Procter & Gamble. But you'd be wrong. Duncan Hines never baked a cake professionally in his life.

In 1925, Hines was a printing salesman from Kentucky whose business required that he travel all over the country. To ensure that he never accidentally returned to those places that served, in his words, "library paste... as gravy," he began taking notes on every restaurant at which he ate. In 1935 he printed a list of his favorite restaurants on the back of his Christmas cards. Word of the list spread so widely that Hines began to get requests for the cards from strangers. When a $1 levy failed to stem the tide of mail, Hines decided to publish a pocket guidebook of his opinions called "Adventures in Good Eating." To ensure the integrity of everything he wrote, Hines never accepted free meals or lodging or charged anyone for a listing.

With automobile travel then coming into its own, people were hungry for this information. And the way Hines wrote about it was so entertaining ("If the soup had been as warm as the wine; if the wine had been as old as the turkey; and if the turkey had had a breast like the maid, it would have been a swell dinner" was one of his lines) that the little book soon sold more than a quarter of a million copies and eventually went through 46 editions. A restaurant's pride was to be able to post a sign that read, "Recommended by Duncan Hines." A survey of housewives in the late 1940s concluded that Duncan Hines was the most trusted name in food and also better known than incumbent Vice President Alben Barkley—even in Barkley's home state of Kentucky!

Other books, covering lodging and vacation spots, soon followed. To write and update them, Duncan traveled more than 50,000 miles a year and sometimes ate as many as six meals a day. (Miraculously, articles of the time say he was only "slightly on the rotund side.") At the time of his death, in 1958, he had two offices and a staff of 55 to help with evaluations and the more than 1,000 letters he received each day.

All this was possible because of the way Hines capitalized on his fame by endorsing kitchen equipment and hundreds of food products, including, in 1948, cake mixes made by the Hines-Park Company, which he formed with business partner Roy Park. (He apparently saw non-restaurant products as beyond the scope of his ethical code.) Within three weeks of its introduction, Duncan Hines had captured 48 percent of the cake mix market. Consumers literally ate his mixes up.

In the 1930s and '40s, Duncan Hines was America's foremost restaurant critic. Although he never accepted free meals or charged anyone for a listing, he did endorse hundreds of appliances and food products, including baking mixes that are still made by Procter & Gamble.

In 1956, Procter & Gamble bought the Hines-Park Company and exclusive rights to the Duncan Hines name. Shortly afterward, Duncan Hines's restaurant endorsement signs were changed to resemble the trademark symbol still used on the cake packages.

Today if someone saw a sign that said, "Recommended by Duncan Hines," however, they'd surmise—probably correctly—that it was for no other reason than that the product was made by Procter & Gamble.

THE CONTROVERSIAL AUNT JEMIMA

Is she the smiling symbol of Southern hospitality and good cooking or a stereotypic depiction of the black woman as a fat, happy mammy, eager to do the bidding of her white owner? After more than 100 years, Aunt Jemima has come to symbolize both these things—as well as one of the most popular lines of pancake and waffle products in the supermarket.

Like most controversial depictions of black Americans, Aunt Jemima was the creation of a white man. Mill owner Chris Rutt of St. Joseph, Missouri, invented the first pancake mix as a way of ensuring sales of his flour in a city overrun with flour mills. He got the idea for the trademark when he attended a minstrel show in 1889 and saw blackface comedians (one of whom was wearing the Southern cook's uniform of an apron and a red bandanna) perform a show-stopping New Orleans-style cakewalk to a tune called "Aunt Jemima." Rutt decided to appropriate the name and the look, trying to link the tradition of great Southern cooking with his pancake product.

When Rutt and partner Charles Underwood sold the company shortly afterward, the trademark was embraced by new owner R. T. Davis of the Davis Milling Company. If Rutt had invented pancake mix and given it its name, Davis was the one who had the then entirely novel idea that Aunt Jemima should be brought to life. After inquiring around town for anyone who knew of a personable black woman who was also a good cook, Davis found Nancy Green, a judge's maid and former slave who seemed to fit all his criteria. Green was seen for the first time at the Chicago World's Fair of 1893. There, Davis set up a huge display in the shape of a flour barrel. Outside the barrel, near the front, Nancy Green was Aunt Jemima: cooking pancakes, singing songs, telling stories, greeting fair visitors and handing out souvenir buttons that bore her likeness and read, "I'se in town, honey!" Green's popularity at the fair rivaled the Midway belly dancer, Little Egypt, and before long special details of police had to be assigned to control the crowds at the Davis exhibit. Among the throng were buyers who placed more than 50,000 orders for Aunt Jemima pancake mix. Green never returned to cleaning house for the judge.

The Davis Company also began a box-top premium campaign offering an Aunt Jemima rag doll (and subsequently, a whole family of "comic pickaninnies") to anyone who sent in one proof of purchase and 25 cents. Many black girls did, and in their daily exposure to the dolls, grew to aspire to be black domestics too.

But this is twentieth-century thinking. Davis knew only that both of these schemes were successful. As a result, in subsequent years his company turned to new promotions whenever they had a sales problem. During World War I, sales dropped alarmingly when government rationing of wheat flour forced the company to temporarily use a blend of flours the public didn't like. To help win customers back, the J. Walter Thompson advertising agency spun a series of exciting—but entirely fictitious—stories about Aunt Jemima's life in the South. One ad showed Aunt Jemima watching in horror as a Mississippi steamboat burned (the copy beneath explained how the wreck's survivors found their way to Aunt Jemima's cabin and were fed platefuls of steaming pancakes). Another showed Davis executives visiting that same cabin to negotiate the sale of her secret pancake recipe.

When sales declined during the Depression, the business (now owned by Quaker Oats) decided to bring Aunt Jemima to life once again in the guise of a 350-pound Chicago woman named Anna Robinson. Her main job was to be photographed making pancakes with stars from stage and screen. Her smile was so warm and infectious that company officials decided to capture it in a redesign of the Aunt Jemima logo.

Two other women portrayed Aunt Jemima: Edith Wilson, on TV and radio, and Aylene Lewis, at the Aunt Jemima Kitchen at Disneyland. By the mid-1960s, the practice of impersonating Aunt Jemima was dropped entirely, as were all Aunt Jemima premiums, in response to objections from Civil Rights era blacks who viewed her as a prop that helped to enforce ideas of racial inferiority. Most of all, blacks hated her kerchief: in derision, some even called her Handkerchief Head. Threatened with boycotts by the black community, Aunt Jemima lost her kerchief as well as about 100 pounds and 40 years in the redesign of 1968, although vestiges of the kerchief—in the form of a red headband—remained.

The Aunt Jemima portrait that is seen on packages today wears no headgear at all. Her perm, pearl earrings and lace collar give her an air of prosperity. During the research that accompanied the debut of the new drawing in 1989, consumers said they saw a young grandmother who works, is active in her church and likes to cook. Busy as she is, she's probably also the type of person who appreciates the convenience of many of the microwave, frozen and other breakfast convenience products now sold under her name.

JELL-O: A LOT MORE THAN SKIN AND BONES

When you get down to essentials, Jell-O is basically the glutinous material from animal bone, skin and connective tissue combined with colored and flavored sugar. The only difference between gelatin such as Jell-O and glue is their degree of purity.

And yet, Jell-O is the savior of the sickroom and a major ingredient in more than 1,700 published recipes. It is, in fact, America's largest-selling prepared dessert. How can this be explained? Could it be Jell-O's taste, its ease in blending with other ingredients, its famous wiggle-jiggle, the effective marketing campaigns that have accompanied its sales through the years? Or could it be simply that hardly anyone ever talks about what Jell-O is really made of?

The first mention of the jellylike properties of boiled bones was made as far back as 1682. In 1865 an American inventor named Peter Cooper obtained the first patent on a gelatin dessert, but it took a former carpenter named Pearl B. Wait of LeRoy, New York, to see its commercial possibilities. Wait had specialized in selling patent medicines—his most successful product was a cough syrup—and in 1897 he decided to try peddling a flavored version of Cooper's dessert. Wait's wife, May, gave the product its name—whether it was because she didn't know gelatin started with a *g* or because the product had to jell before being eaten, no one is sure. The sound *O* was a popular ending for food products at the time.

In fact, Wait's neighbor, inventor Orator Woodward, had found some success marketing a Postum-like grain-based cereal drink he called Grain-O. (Certainly it brought Woodward more income than one of his early creations: a cement nest egg infused with a medicine that killed lice on chickens.) When sales of Jell-O lagged and Wait wanted to sell out for $450, Woodward bought. Didn't he have a food manufacturing and distribution system already set up?

True enough, but that didn't mean people were any more inclined to buy Jell-O. In fact, during that first year, Woodward was walking through his plant with his superintendent, A. S. Nico, when, regarding a storage section piled high with unsold cases of Jell-O, Woodward offered to sell Nico the whole Jell-O business for

$35. Nico refused.

Woodward soon had cause to be glad of that answer and Nico to weep. By 1902, Jell-O sales had climbed to $250,000 a year. A few years after Woodward's son took over in 1904 and began promoting the product in a big way, sales were just under $1 million.

The early ads gave some clue to Jell-O's appeal. They showed women in fashionable attire, displaying Jell-O on silver trays or in expensive, fluted glassware. The first in a long series of Jell-O booklets offered testimonials to the dessert from actress Ethel Barrymore and opera singer Madame Ernestine Schumann-Heink. The point was to show women they need not be stuck living in the rough-hued way of their prairie forebears. Like the actress and opera stars, they too could eat one of the finest, most delicate desserts made.

In 1904, a product trademark also was employed. She was the Jell-O girl, the cute little daughter of the artist who had been hired to come up with the trademark. Although company officials didn't like Franklin King's drawings, they liked the real-life model who inspired him. Photographs of King's daughter were used in advertisements from 1904 through 1908. In 1908, Kewpie doll creator Rose O'Neill was hired to create a drawing of the Jell-O girl for the Jell-O package. Many other famous artists illustrated Jell-O advertisements and recipe books, including Maxfield Parrish and Norman Rockwell.

While many companies were then advertising, Jell-O was one of the first to do mass mailings. The company also hired a force of spiffily attired salesmen to travel the countryside in horse and buggy and spread the word about the new food. At country fairs and women's club meetings these men would show how to make Jell-O, then pass out free samples and cookbooks.

Recipes continue to be a popular reason for buying Jell-O. It's rare to pick up a community cookbook or go to a church supper that does not feature at least one dish using Jell-O. There's something about the way Jell-O turns from liquid to solid that makes it highly adaptable to all kinds of cooking and inspiring to creative cooks. Two classic recipes are the Jell-O Poke cake (where unset Jell-O is poured over a cake poked full of holes) and Jell-O Broken Glass (where different-colored cubes of Jell-O held together with Cool Whip lend a stained glass window effect). The latest rage among Jell-O-philes is to take Gummi candy creatures and float them in Jell-O dioramas that rival the work of the great ice sculptors. One example is the Jell-O-filled fish tank implanted with Gummi Bear fish and parsley seaweed.

Sales of Jell-O as a serious foodstuff fell after 1968. In a time of protest against the Vietnam War, Jell-O was equated with the establishment and corporate America. No one made the point more clearly than playwright LeRoi Jones in his play *Jell-O*. In this vitriolic spoof of Jack Benny's popular Jell-O-sponsored radio show of the 1930s and 1940s, Rochester robs and beats up Jack Benny and Mary Livingston in a race conflict.

Others thought Jell-O was merely déclassé. Proof is in the way it was served on the blue-collar situation comedies "All in the Family" and "Roseanne." And can it be an accident that lime Jell-O was the favorite medium for novelty wrestlers to cavort in during the 1980s? The fact that Jell-O is 80 to 90 percent sugar and artificial flavors didn't endear it to the growing numbers of Americans who were concerned about the nutritional value of the food they were eating.

Between 1968 and 1989, sales of gelatin desserts declined 57 percent. But Jell-O put a stop to that in 1990 when it promoted the idea of adding one-third less water to the Jell-O powder to create a firm, candy-like treat that kids could cut with cookie cutters, then eat with their hands. In the spring of 1990, General Foods was receiving up to 200 calls a day requesting the so-called Jigglers recipe and Jell-O sales were up one quarter over the previous year.

The dessert also achieved a certain amount of respectability that year when the Smithsonian Institution held a conference about Jell-O history (although it should be noted that it was held on April Fools' Day). Among the many lectures given was one by Rayna Green of the museum's Native American Indian program titled: "White Religious Cults: Lime Jell-O and Little Marshmallows."

A Nestlé's Morsel Of Sweetness

The idea that putting together various combinations of cookies, candy, cake or ice cream could create treats even more tasty than any one of these alone might seem self-evident in these days of Heath Bar Crunch ice cream and caramelized brownies, but it took a great mind to think of it in the first place. That mind belonged to Ruth Wakefield, the inventor—indirectly—of Nestlé's Semi-Sweet Chocolate Morsels.

In 1930, Wakefield was resident baker and co-owner, with her husband, of a historic inn on the outskirts of Whitman, Massachusetts. It was called the Toll House

because in colonial days it was across the street from the tollgate of the old Boston-New Bedford Turnpike.

One day Wakefield was preparing a batch of butter drop cookies when she discovered she did not have nuts to put in. She decided to break up a Nestlé Semi-Sweet Chocolate Bar into pieces and use them instead. Wakefield expected to end up with chocolate cookies. She was surprised and pleased to find that instead of melting and spreading, the chocolate had softened to a deliciously creamy texture. The resulting creation, which she dubbed Chocolate Crispies, became very popular at her inn, and when her recipe was published in a Boston newspaper, around New England as well. Regional sales of the Nestlé bar skyrocketed.

Eventually Wakefield approached the Nestlé Company and reached an agreement that allowed them to print her Toll House Cookie recipe on the wrapper of their Semi-Sweet Chocolate Bar in exchange for supplying her with all the chocolate she could use to make her cookies for the rest of her life (among other things). They called them Toll House Cookies after her inn, which was quite well known for its fine cooking and hospitality.

Soon Nestlé began scoring the bar and packaged it with a chopper for cutting it into small pieces. In 1939, Nestlé's sold its first bag of morsels. (Like most companies making chocolate bits, Nestlé recently came out with a bag of chocolate chunks—chocolate pieces of a size that is probably closer to the candy bar pieces Wakefield used.)

Ruth Wakefield retired in 1967, and later her Toll House Inn burned to the ground. But her cookie creation has continued to grow in popularity, with Nestlé's production of the morsels increasing by 100 million

---

The Original Toll House Cookies

1 cup plus 2 teaspoons sifted flour
½ teaspoon baking soda
½ teaspoon salt
½ cup soft butter or shortening
6 tablespoons granulated sugar
6 tablespoons firmly packed brown sugar
½ teaspoon vanilla
¼ teaspoon water
1 egg
1 cup Nestlé Toll House Semi-Sweet Chocolate Morsels
½ cup coarsely chopped walnuts

Sift together flour, baking soda, salt; set aside. Combine in bowl butter, granulated and brown sugars, vanilla and water; beat until creamy. Beat in egg. Add flour mixture and mix well. Stir in chocolate morsels and walnuts. Drop by well-rounded half teaspoonfuls onto greased cookie sheet. Bake at 375 degrees for 10 to 12 minutes. Makes 50 cookies.

---

per day between 1979 and 1987. Her Chocolate Crispies also have been the inspiration for an entire cookie-making industry and the fortunes of such leaders in the field as Mrs. Fields, Famous Amos and David.

In 1979, Nestlé's 40-year agreement with Ruth Wakefield expired, and for the first time, the company was able to change the recipe on the back of the morsel bags. Of course, her original recipe has spawned countless variations (that's why they're called by the generic term chocolate chip cookies rather than the specific Toll House) but this was the first time Nestlé had modified it. Although most of the changes were slight (shortening the baking time, omitting the need to grease the pans and sift the flour), there are some who believe that Wakefield's recipe produces the better cookie.

CRISCO: THE NEW SCIENCE OF BAKING AND FRYING

Modern consumers have become very used to eating the products of science. We drink grape soda and eat Cheez Doodles and green bagels on St. Patrick's Day all without batting an eye and usually also without realizing that the granddaddy of all scientific foods is Procter & Gamble's humble Crisco vegetable shortening.

At the turn of the century, P&G was primarily known as a soap maker. While soap and vegetable shortening might be miles apart in the supermarket, both are made by manipulating oils. When P&G executives learned of some research being done in Europe in which oil was being turned into a partially solid product through hydrogenation (adding hydrogen), they decided to use the process to convert vegetable oil into a substitute for the natural shortenings, lard and butter. Testing on the new product, which they called Crisco (a combination of two other name candidates, Krispo and Cryst, which were supposed to suggest the sound of hissing fat), revealed the following advantages over lard and butter:

- It did not go rancid as quickly;
- It could stand a higher temperature than the other cooking fats and therefore didn't smoke up the kitchen as easily;
- It cost less;
- It fried quicker, and foods fried in it absorbed less fat;
- It could be used equally well for making cakes, pie crusts or bread.

Given all this, you might think that housewives would have rushed to stores to buy Crisco when it first came out in the spring of 1911. The very first ads, in fact, confidently predicted Crisco was "a Scientific Discovery Which Will Affect Every Kitchen in America." But when P&G decided to invite groups of women into their plant to lunch on foods made with Crisco, they found few who would accept the free gift of a 1½-pound can of Crisco. It wasn't that the lunch didn't taste good—it's just that their mothers had taught them to cook with butter and lard. And what did a soap company know about making food anyway?

Officials at P&G realized that if they ever hoped to sell Crisco, they were going to have to do something dramatic to make the American housewife see its

Convincing Mother

At first she and her family are satisfied with the shortening they always have used. It *is* pretty hard to improve upon her pie crust and cake.

But someone induces her to *try* Crisco. Perhaps it is her daughter who has used it at Domestic Science School, or a neighbor who has obtained excellent results.

After the first trial, the old fashioned cook slowly but surely comes to use Crisco for all cooking. She has become a Crisco enthusiast. She has found these advantages in using

For Frying—For Shortening
For Cake Making

Frying

There is no smoke nor odor. Fried foods are free from the taste of grease. They now are tasty and crisp. They are made more digestible, for Crisco is all vegetable. The same Crisco can be used to fry fish, onions, doughnuts, etc., merely by straining out the food particles after each frying.

Shortening

Crisco gives pastry a new flakiness and digestibility. Crisco always is of the same freshness and consistency. Its uniform quality makes for uniform results.

Cake Making

Crisco gives richness at smaller cost. It brings cake making back to popularity. Butter bills are reduced and cakes stay fresh and moist longer.

Marion Harris Neil, Cookery Editor, Ladies' Home Journal, has prepared a New Crisco Cook Book. This is printed in two editions. One book contains 250 recipes and is free. The other contains 615 recipes and a "Calendar of Dinners," and may be had for five 2-cent stamps. The Calendar tells *what* to eat every day of the year, and the recipes tell how to economically prepare these new and delightful foods. For either of these books address Dept. E-2, The Procter & Gamble Co., Cincinnati.

advantages. The Company decided to hire six home economists to cook Crisco before audiences in the largest auditoriums around the country. Probably most of the women who attended these week-long "cooking schools" didn't even know they were sponsored by Crisco because they were never advertised that way. Although Crisco would be displayed prominently on the demonstration table, the home economists were told not to mention it until—as inevitably happened—someone in the audience asked about the shortening they were using. The real purpose of the lectures was also muddled by the deal P&G made with local newspapers: In exchange for agreeing to publicize the lectures, the demonstrations would be called the Tribune Cooking School or Herald Cooking School. At a time when cooking schools were mainly the province of the wealthy, newspapers scored big public relations points by giving the average woman the chance to attend the lecture-demonstrations. Each of the home economists traveled about nine months of the year, then retreated to P&G headquarters to develop next year's class. Each had a devoted following.

Crisco also was promoted through more conventional methods such as magazine and newspaper advertising, cookbooks (a cooking pamphlet was attached to the very first cans of Crisco) and radio spots (the first, in 1923, consisted entirely of Crisco cake and cookie recipes read over the air). Although all these things helped, what really broke down housewives' resistance was the start of World War I and the resulting shortage in lard. Suddenly buying Crisco was the patriotic thing to do, and Crisco took advantage of the situation by printing Food Administration slogans in their ads.

Today Crisco is a baking staple as accepted as flour and baking soda—at least when it comes to baking pie crusts. Despite recent concerns about fat and cholesterol and the introduction of Butter Flavor Crisco in 1981, most people still prefer to make their cakes and cookies with butter and margarine.

Morton Salt: When It Rains, It Pours

Almost no brand of salt cakes in humid weather anymore. But when the Morton Salt Company first came out with free-flowing salt in 1912, clumpy salt was as big a culinary problem as hard brown sugar is today. (Morton solved the problem by adding a small quantity of the anti-caking agent magnesium carbonate; today, sodium silico aluminate serves much the same function.) So the picture of a little girl walking in the rain with a package of salt spilling behind her coupled with the slogan, "When it rains, it pours," seemed the perfect way to distinguish their salt from all the others.

Company namesake Joy Morton—son of Arbor Day founder and onetime U.S. Secretary of Agriculture Sterling Morton—was working as a teller in a Chicago bank when he decided to invest $10,000 to become a partner in the locally based E. I. Wheeler Salt Company. When Wheeler died in 1885, Morton became president, brought his brother into the company and renamed the firm Jay Morton & Co.

Like most salt companies of the day, Morton did the bulk of its business with food-service, industrial, agricultural and highway concerns. Nevertheless, in 1911, it decided to introduce a free-flowing salt in a never-before-used round cardboard tube package. To get the word out on the new product, Morton introduced another salt industry first: consumer advertising. They hired the N. W. Ayer agency to prepare 12 advertisements for *Good Housekeeping* magazine. When Sterling Morton II, Joy's son and now an executive of the company, reviewed the proposed advertisements, he was particularly drawn to a backup sketch of the now-famous little girl.

"Perhaps the fact that my daughter Suzette was occupying a great deal of my attention at that time had something to do with my interest," Sterling later said. Sterling Morton and agency executives brainstormed to whittle the phrase that had been placed underneath the picture—"Even in rainy weather it flows freely"—to the more succinct and catchy "When it rains, it pours." After running in *Good Housekeeping*, the picture and slogan were placed on the label in 1914.

The picture of the little girl has been revised five times since then, most recently in 1968. The changes have usually been to make her hairstyle and dress look more up-to-date. But she has yet to wear slacks. And even after all these years, she still seems oblivious to the fact that the salt package she is carrying is open and leaking.

SOFT DRINKS AND JUICES

DR PEPPER: WOULDN'T YOU LIKE TO BE A WEIRDO TOO?

Are you a woman who wears hats? A man who doesn't like sports? An employee who's not afraid to speak his mind to the boss? Then maybe you're a Pepper.

A Pepper is somebody who's not afraid to order a Dr Pepper when most of the rest of the world is having Coke or Pepsi. It's somebody who's crazy about Dr Pepper's blend of 23 ingredients—even when they have no idea what those 23 ingredients are.

The Dr Pepper recipe is a big secret that's known to only four people inside Dr Pepper's Dallas headquarters and is locked up in two different city banks (in case some disaster were to destroy one of them). The company will only say that it does not contain cherry, cola or, as is rumored by wary children, prune juice.

Given the impressive number of ingredients, is it any wonder that Dr Pepper was created by a pharmacist? His name was Charles Alderton, and he worked at Wade Morrison's Old Corner Drug Store in Waco, Texas. In between filling prescriptions, Alderton worked the soda fountain and one day came up with a fruit-flavored drink that caught on with Morrison's customers. Morrison had come to Texas after being fired from a pharmacy in Virginia because he was courting the owner's daughter. Customers had heard of Wade's lost love so often that they suggested naming the new drink after the Virginia pharmacy's owner, Dr. Charles Pepper.

The drink didn't advance the romance—Morrison ended up marrying a woman who lived in Waco. But the drink sold so well that Morrison formed a partnership with a local beverage chemist named Robert S. Lazenby to begin bottling it. In 1904, Lazenby and his son-in-law, J. B. O'Hara, unveiled Dr Pepper at the 1904 St. Louis World's Fair. Ice cream cones, hamburgers and hot dog buns were also all introduced there.

Dr Pepper remained a Southwestern drink until the mid-1920s, when someone in the company came across a book by Columbia University nutrition professor Walter Eddy that recommended people take a shot of sugar to boost energy at 10 a.m., 2 p.m. and 4 p.m. The Dr Pepper company immediately put "Drink a Bite to Eat at 10, 2 and 4" on its bottles, and Americans began doing just that. The slogan became so familiar that the company soon reduced it to simply a clock symbol with three hands pointing to those hours. A similar striving for simplification left the Dr. of the Dr Pepper logo without its period in 1960.

In the 1960s and 1970s, thanks to a series of advertising campaigns owning up to its weirdness (one calling it, "The world's most misunderstood soft drink," others explaining that despite the name, it didn't taste like medicine), Dr Pepper became one of America's five top-selling soft drinks. You probably didn't think there were that many offbeat people out there, did you?

HIRES ROOT BEER: TEA IS FOR WIMPS

The word *root beer*, like *turkey shoot* and *sweet bread*, seems designed to make people who are learning English as a second language wish they could pack it up and move back to wherever they came from. In many cases inappropriate or confusing words and phrases come about by accident or misuse, but giving the name root beer to a product that contained no alcohol was an intentional deception by Charles Hires, inventor of the first and most famous root beer soda pop.

Hires, 24 and a Philadelphia pharmacist, was on his honeymoon in 1875 when the innkeeper's wife at the rural New Jersey inn where he and his bride were staying served them an herb tea containing, among other things, juniper, wintergreen and sarsaparilla. Although it was an old recipe in the innkeeper's family, root and berry drinks like it had been made by American Indians for hundreds of years.

Like most druggists of the time, Hires mixed and sold carbonated beverages at the counter of his store. But he had never tasted anything like the New Jersey woman's drink. When he returned to Philadelphia, he asked two college professors for help in developing a formula for a powder that, when mixed with water, sugar and yeast, could reproduce the taste.

A devout Quaker, Hires had hopes of selling his Hires Root Tea to hard-drinking Pennsylvania miners, thus putting them on the path to salvation. If this was his mission, a friend told him, he must change the name. "The miners will never drink it if it were called a tea. Better call it root beer."

In 1876, Hires handed out free glasses of his drink at the Philadelphia Centennial Exposition. The response was so encouraging that he decided to expand his marketing plans beyond the coal miners. Soon Hires began advertising in newspapers and magazines and on trade cards and metal serving trays. Many of these featured pictures of plump, rosy-cheeked children (the unstated assumption was that the children got that way by drinking root beer). In keeping with his evangelistic leanings, other ads featured religious paintings and appropriate scriptural sayings. An 1891 ad claimed, "Hires Rootbeer gives the children strength to resist the enervating effects of the heat, bridges the convalescent over the trying part of a hot day, helps even a cynic to see the brighter side of life."

Hires needed a positive attitude in 1895. That year the Women's Christian Temperance Union called for a nationwide boycott of Hires, which they believed to be a beer. The women didn't back off until 1898, when an independent laboratory test determined that a bottle of Hires contained only about as much alcohol as a loaf of bread. Sales of the powdered, liquid-extract and bottled forms of Hires Root Beer promptly returned to normal and eventually made Hires a millionaire. (Although the powdered form has long been gone, the liquid extract was sold until 1983.)

Hires remained president of the firm until 1923 and continued as chairman until his death 12 years later, but like Jeno's and Chun King founder Jeno Paulucci, he was apparently not satisfied with simply one big food success. In 1896, Hires began condensing milk at a Pennsylvania plant, the start of a company that grew to 23 plants in four states and Canada. When he sold this business to Nestlé in 1918, that deal earned him another million.

7-UP: THE UNLIKELY SUCCESS OF THE UNCOLA

You would think an advertising and marketing man would know better than to give a new product a name as unwieldy as "Bib-Label Lithiated Lemon-Lime Soda." To bring a new lemon-lime soda on the market when there were already more than 600 available and to price it higher than the others didn't seem so smart either. Then to introduce it into supermarkets just two weeks before the great stock market crash of 1929—it all seemed to add up to a recipe for disaster.

Instead, Bib-Label Lithiated Lemon-Lime Soda went on to become one of the most popular soft drinks in America, 7-Up. How did it make it?

Early ads, like many food ads of the time, promoted 7-Up as a health drink. Its creator, C. L. Griggs, seemed to think 7-Up's primary asset was its carbonation—or "life gas"—which he recommended as a cure for everything from car sickness to hangovers and indigestion. But the real reason 7-Up lived up to its slogan, "Takes the Ouch Out of the Grouch," was probably the ingredient lithium—a powerful drug now used to treat

manic-depressives. Lithium remained on the label until the mid-1940s, when 7-Up was already well on the way to being one of America's favorite soft drinks.

No doubt the name change also helped. The date of the change is as fuzzy as the reason behind it. Most sources attribute the 7 to the size of the bottle at the time—7 ounces. But one company executive says it's because the 7-Up taste is created by blending seven natural flavors. Several theorize the "Up" had something to do with the drink's extreme carbonation. In fact, bubbles originally surrounded the trademark. Another said it refers to the old drinking expression "Bottoms up," and still another that Griggs borrowed the word from another soda made in St. Louis at the time called Bubbles Up. But recent 7-Up scholarship reveals the name had more to do with Grigg's long admiration of cattle brands as a simple and clear method of identification. Reading a newspaper article about several cattle brands, Griggs saw a reference to one that consisted of the numeral 7 with an adjacent letter *u*. So cattle were the real inspiration for the 7-Up name.

In 1968, a highly successful advertising campaign starring actor Geoffrey Holder gave 7-Up another name: the Uncola. The Seven-Up Company merged with Dr Pepper in 1986, and like Dr Pepper's "The World's Most Misunderstood Soft Drink" campaign, 7-

Up's Uncola ads promoted as asset the thing that everyone had always identified as weakness: the fact that it wasn't a cola in a country where colas had long been the most popular soft drinks. To drive the point home, 7-Up even came out with upside-down, Coke-style fountain glasses. The psychedelic graphics featured in the Uncola ads helped to make the soda more appealing to the rock-and-roll generation, although they might have liked it even better if it had still contained lithium! 7-Up was also the first major soft drink to call attention to its lack of caffeine. It also contains no artificial colors or flavors.

But real fans of 7-Up—like real fans of Coca-Cola, Pepsi and Dr Pepper—don't merely drink their favorite soda. They cook with it too. Marilyn Ingram, a home

economist based in Dallas, once developed 150 recipes using 7-Up. Her three favorites are 7-Up pound cake, 7-Up baked beans and 7-Up pancakes. To make lighter pancakes, simply substitute 7-Up for the liquid specified for any pancake mix. (The other two recipes are given below.)

Two times a year for the past eight years, a television news show in Greenville, South Carolina, has run a 15-minute cooking segment devoted solely to 7-Up recipes. In the spring, the segment has either an Easter or a bridal theme. In November, it's about holiday cooking with the soft drink. During the 1989 holiday season, more than 8,000 viewers wrote in for recipes.

7-Up Baked Beans

3 cans (1 lb. each) pork and beans
1 medium onion, finely chopped
¼ cup light molasses
3 tablespoons pickle relish
1 tablespoon Worcestershire sauce
2 teaspoons prepared mustard
1 bottle (7 oz.) 7-Up
1 can (2 oz.) sliced mushrooms, drained

Combine pork and beans with all ingredients except mushrooms and place in a 2-quart casserole dish. Bake uncovered in a 325 degree oven for 1½ hour. Stir in mushrooms and continue baking for ½ hour. Makes 8 to 10 servings.

7-Up Pound Cake

1 stick margarine
1 stick butter
½ cup vegetable shortening
3 cups sugar
5 eggs
3 cups plain flour
1 cup 7-Up
1 tablespoon lemon flavoring
1 tablespoon vanilla flavoring

Preheat oven to 325 degrees. Ingredients should be at room temperature. Cream margarine, butter and shortening with sugar. Add eggs, one at a time, beating well after each. Add flour alternately with 7-Up and flavoring. Bake in a 10-inch greased tube pan at 325 degrees for at least 1 hour and 10 minutes.

COKE IS IT (PART OF AMERICANA, THAT IS)

When Coca-Cola was introduced in Italy, one newspaper claimed it had "the taste of a damp rag for cleaning floors." Another compared drinking it to "sucking the leg of a recently massaged athlete." Given reviews like that you might wonder how Coke has become the best-selling soft drink in the world.

Some say it's because of the addictive properties of the caffeine and sugar it contains. Coke is also brewed with coca leaves, but despite what college kids who mixed it with ammonia before final exams as an upper during the 1960s said, all but the most minute trace amounts of cocaine have been removed from the drink. (Even the original formula had so little that one chemist said you would have had to consume five-and-a-half quarts of Coca-Cola to have noticed any physiological effect.) But the Coca-Cola Company's fanaticism about keeping the formula a secret (it's kept in a Georgia bank vault and known only by two or three top executives) has just helped the rumor persist.

The more powerful attraction to Coca-Cola is probably mental and due to the millions of dollars in advertising the company has spent over the years. The ad that assembled teenage Coca-Cola drinkers from around the world on a Roman hillside to sing "I'd Like to Teach the World to Sing" was so popular a noncommercial version of it became a top-40 hit. (In 1990 Coca-Cola hired the Pinkerton Detective Agency to find the then grown-up teens and revived the ad with them singing with *their* kids.) A 1979 Coca-Cola ad that showed the soft side of Pittsburgh Steeler Mean Joe Green inspired the NBC-TV movie *The Steeler and the Pittsburgh Kid*, the first-ever feature film to be based on a commercial.

The legend is that Atlanta pharmacist John Styth Pemberton stirred up the first-ever batch of Coca-Cola with an oar in a huge iron kettle in his backyard in 1886. Before he added caramel coloring, the product had a greenish tinge. Pemberton had already invented such concoctions as Triplex liver pills and Globe of Flower cough medicine and, having that bent of mind, marketed his new drink as a cure for hangover and stomach upset.

Knowing that the soft drink contained flavorings from both the kola nut and coca leaves, Pemberton's bookkeeper, Frank Robinson, gave the product its name and its script logo—Robinson was supposedly a stickler for good penmanship. The distinctive Mae West-shaped bottle was introduced later, in 1915, to help distinguish Coca-Cola from its many imitators—even in the dark. The winning design was based, appropriately enough, on the shape of a kola nut.

By the time another Atlanta pharmacist, Asa Candler, bought the right to make Coca-Cola from Pemberton in 1891 (for approximately $2,000), patent medicines in general and drugs such as cocaine in particular were beginning to come under fire from citizens and the Federal Drug Administration. Pemberton hadn't had much success selling Coca-Cola as a medicine anyway (he'd cleared only about $50 after advertising his first year), so Candler began an all-out advertising blitz to sell Coke as a recreational drink.

Calling Coca-Cola "delicious and refreshing" and never Coke (the company battled the use of the popular nickname in ads until 1941, when they finally gave in), Candler commissioned pictures of robust women drinking it and placed the pictures on serving trays, mirrors and signs. Such forms of advertising were not common then. As farsighted as Candler was about advertising, he could not see selling his product anywhere but in pharmacy soda fountains. So when two Chattanooga lawyers approached him about securing the rights to bottle Coca-Cola, he gave it to them for only one dollar.

Candler went on to become mayor of Atlanta in 1916. Not long afterward, his family sold the remainder of their rights to Coca-Cola to a group of investors led by financier Ernest Woodruff for $25 million—making it the largest business transaction to have taken place in the South until that time. After World War I, sugar prices reached record highs and resulted in a few rough years for the company. But when World War II was declared, then-president Robert Woodruff (Ernest's son) went on the offensive, declaring, "We will see that every man in uniform gets a bottle of Coca-Cola for 5 cents wherever he is and wherever he goes." It sounded selfless and patriotic, but it resulted in American taxpayers helping to pay Coke to ship bottling machinery to the front. By the end of the war, most GIs were devoted Coke drinkers, and Coke had the beginnings of a system to sell the drink worldwide.

Coke is the first English word spoken by people in many foreign countries. Coke is also the long-time best-selling soft drink in the United States (although in recent years, the makers of the somewhat sweeter and more citrusy Pepsi-Cola claim to stronger sales in the supermarket.) Coke sales in the South are about double what they are in the rest of the country, and are particularly strong in its home state of Georgia.

But Coke's impact is not just restricted to refreshment. Santa Claus, before Haddon Sundblom's jolly pictures began appearing in Coke's holiday ads during December of 1931, was depicted as a stern, skinny elf.

Because Coke is as much a staple of American kitchens as wine is in French ones, recipes for its use in chocolate cake, pot roast, cleaning toilet bowls and even as a spermicide have spontaneously arisen. (Harvard University researchers checked out the last claim by putting sperm samples in test tubes with different types of Coke. They had some success with Diet Coke but not enough to recommend it as an effective form of birth control.) Coke's legacy to American life is explored at The World of Coca-Cola, a museum at 55 Martin Luther King Drive in Atlanta, Georgia 30303-3505 (404-676-5151), which features, among other things, free drinks, a jukebox that will play such songs as "When the Dodo Bird Is Singing in the Coca-Cola Tree" and a specially constructed can of Coke that was carried aboard the space shuttle in 1985. There's also a Coca-Cola memorabilia store, Coca-Cola Fifth Avenue, at 711 Fifth Avenue in New York City.

Coke officials seem to have forgotten how much their soda had become part of American culture when they announced a change of formula in April 1985. Consumers in blind taste tests said they preferred the new formula, but the public was outraged that Coke officials were messing with their drink. During the controversy, Coke's consumer line got 1,500 calls of protest per day and one group calling itself the Old Coke Drinkers of America threatened to sue. Three months later Coke acknowledged its mistake and announced the return of old Coke as Coke Classic. Network ABC considered the news so important it interrupted its regular programming to make the announcement. By 1991, the market share of New Coke was measured at less than 1 percent. Undeterred, the company began reintroducing New Coke under the new name, Coke II.

The Pepsi Challenge

Popular wisdom tells us that Democrats drink Coca-Cola and Republicans drink Pepsi. It only follows, then, that as conservative Republicans dominated the American political scene in the late 1980s and early 1990s, Pepsi came closer to its long-time goal of displacing Coke as the most popular soft drink in America than at any other time in its history.

But Pepsi came close to oblivion several times. During the Depression, when the company was having a particularly difficult financial time, Pepsi-Cola was actually offered for sale to the Coca-Cola Company.

In 1890, Brad's Drink was one of dozens of colas on the market in the wake of Coca-Cola's early success. Brad was Caleb D. Bradham, a North Carolina pharmacist, but it wasn't long before he changed the name of his drink to Pepsi—after dyspepsia, or upset stomach, the ailment he claimed it could soothe. Because he wrote the name of his drink in script closely imitative of Coca-Cola's, Pepsi-Cola seemed even more of a rip-off than some others. After a good start (he had franchised more than 200 bottling plants by 1906), Bradham's business became one of many casualties of World War I. As a hedge against further inflation, Bradham had stockpiled sugar at the outrageous postwar price of 22 cents a pound. When sugar prices dropped to three cents a pound in December 1920, he was in deep financial trouble.

To the rescue came Charles Guth, a candy shop owner who bought so much syrup from Coke that he thought he deserved to get it at a wholesale price. When Coke disagreed, he took his business to Pepsi. Eventually Guth ended up buying the financially troubled company. When Coke executives found out that Guth's Loft Candy Store customers were asking for Coke but being served Pepsi without any kind of disclaimer, Coke took Guth to court—the first of many times Coke would sue its rival.

The cost of defending itself against this charge combined with the Depression's impact on business nearly did Pepsi in once again. In desperation, Guth came up with the crazy idea of filling old 12-oz. beer bottles full of Pepsi and selling them for five cents—the price of a six-oz. bottle of Coke. To promote this bargain, the company hired a skywriting plane to spell out "Drink Pepsi-Cola" above New York City (an advertising technique the company still employs today) and, more importantly, paid two advertising men $2,500 to write this jingle to the tune of the old English hunting song "D'ye Know John Peel?":

> *Pepsi-Cola hits the spot;*
> *Twelve full ounces, that's a lot.*
> *Twice as much for a nickel, too;*
> *Pepsi-Cola is the drink for you.*

In 1940, the radio industry said there was only one song Americans knew better: "The Star-Spangled Banner."

But when economic conditions improved, Pepsi's cheap image became more liability than asset. In fact, some people would pour Pepsi into old Coke bottles before serving it to guests. Promotional appearances by actress Joan Crawford, who happened to be married to Pepsi president Alfred Steele, helped elevate the brand's image. So did a new advertising campaign. Since Pepsi couldn't claim Coke's hold on the American establishment, Pepsi began to cultivate an image as the choice of the new generation or, as 1953 ads put it, "The Pepsi Generation." Pepsi has returned to this theme time and again, most recently with ads that show rap singer Hammer launching into the schmaltzy song "Feelings" after taking a sip of the supposedly fuddy-duddy Coke.

In the 1970s, Pepsi focused its advertising campaign on the Pepsi Challenge—blind taste tests in which a slight majority of consumers chose Pepsi over Coca-

Cola. Pepsi even put trucks on the road that allowed people to take the Pepsi Challenge in their hometown. When Coke announced it was switching to a new formula in 1985, Pepsi gave its employees a day off to celebrate what they saw as Coke's admission of defeat. When Coke announced they were bringing "old" Coke back, Pepsi ridiculed Coke's blunder in a series of ads showing a confused consumer trying to order a glass of the stuff.

The two colas have also battled in the international arena. In 1959, Pepsi was given exclusive rights to sell cola in the Soviet Union following a Moscow trade fair at which Nikita Khruschev and Vice President Richard Nixon knocked back several bottles of Pepsi. The Senate investigation instigated by Coke officials' screaming revealed that Nixon had once been offered the presidency of a foreign division of Pepsi, and when he decided to join a Wall Street law firm instead had handled the lucrative Pepsi account. But Coke got their revenge when Jimmy Carter became president. Days before China and the United States announced the normalization of relations, Georgian cola maker (and Carter campaign contributor) Coke was granted exclusive cola rights to that huge country.

One of Coke and Pepsi's most recent skirmishes involved non–colored drinks. Just a week after Pepsi officials said they would debut their first national ads for their new Crystal Pepsi during the 1993 Super Bowl, Coke announced plans to come out with Tab Clear.

TANG: ORANGE JUICE FOR ASTRONAUTS

General Foods created Tang to be a fruit-flavored breakfast companion to Instant Maxwell House coffee.

It might have taken a decade, but consumers' initial resistance to instant coffee had by 1955 melted to the point that it now sat in virtually every pantry. General Foods was gambling that the same kind of research, development and marketing that had put instant coffee on the map could persuade people to replace their morning orange juice with a breakfast drink made from water and powder.

The 1950s and 1960s were the era of technological wonders, when food scientists were constantly trying to improve on the properties endowed on food by Mother Nature with such products as Cool Whip and Coffee-mate. In Tang, General Foods sought to create a drink with all the natural nutrients of orange juice that could be stored indefinitely in a cupboard and brought to life with water in an instant.

It took 10 years from the conception of Tang, in 1955, to the time General Foods scientists were actually able to create it. Problems included finding forms of vitamins that would dissolve in water yet stay stable for long periods in a jar. A process developed by Monsanto to keep salt from caking was borrowed to prevent the same thing from happening to Tang. There was also the question of Tang's color. In its natural state Tang was white, but General Foods consumer tests showed people preferred it orange. Scientists had to find coloring agents that would provide the orange color when the powder was dissolved in water.

The product they came up with contained sugar, citric acid (to provide tartness), gum arabic, natural orange flavor, sodium carboxymethylcellulose, calcium phosphate (to prevent caking), sodium citrate, vitamin C, hydrogenated vegetable oil, vitamin A, artificial color, BHA (a preservative) and none of the real orange juice solids Tang contains today.

Just three months after Tang finally achieved national distribution in March of 1965, the National Aeronautics and Space Administration chose Tang to feed the Gemini astronauts in space. Because it didn't spoil, didn't weigh much and was quite nutritious, Tang continued to appear in the Gemini and Apollo galleys through the first moon landing in July 1969. People—especially kids—thrilled to the idea of being able to drink the same thing their heroes did. Commercials (often airing during television news coverage of the space shots) milked the connection for all it was worth.

On earth, consumers found a variety of uses for the product beyond quenching morning thirst. They sprinkled it on hams, used it in cookies and coffee cake and poured it into cake mix batters in place of orange zest. One Midwestern bank official told the company that he substituted Tang for orange juice in his vodka screwdrivers. Dan Aykroyd found dry Tang to be the perfect accompaniment to a breakfast of shredded swine flesh and fried chicken embryos in the Conehead sketches on TV's "Saturday Night Live."

With the diminished interest in the space program and the rising popularity of refrigerated fruit juice blends, Tang has recently fallen on hard times. One industry report showed Tang sales rising a mere 1 percent between 1989 and 1990. But Kraft General Foods has not given up on the race for fruit drink sales any more than NASA has given up on space. In fact, the company recently created a Tang line of fruit juice drinks in cardboard lunchboxes. If today's parents feel nostalgic enough about drinking Tang with the astronauts to buy some for their kids, sales could once again blast off.

WELCH'S GRAPE JUICE: FOR THOSE WHO WILL DRINK NO WINE AT ANY TIME

One of the sweetest of all fruit juices and the one most prone to stain dentures was invented by a dentist. His goal wasn't to drum up more business. He simply was upset that wine was served for communion at his Methodist church.

A devout Methodist and enthusiastic prohibitionist, Dr. Thomas B. Welch wanted to make a nonintoxicating grape-based beverage that would keep his whole congregation from sinning while in church. Living in Vineland, New Jersey, a town that was named for its many vineyards, he had plenty of grapes around to experiment with. In 1869 he enlisted the help of his wife and 17-year-old son in trying to apply the principles of pasteurization to juice from grapes. After cooking the grapes for a few minutes, the trio squeezed the liquid through cloth bags into 12-quart bottles and sealed them with cork and wax. Then Dr. Welch lowered them into boiling water to kill the yeast and, he thought, prevent fermentation. When weeks passed without a single bottle erupting in an explosion, Welch knew he was on to something.

For 20 years, Welch made a small business of selling his grape juice to area churches (Welch's own church, citing the long precedent of using wine, never became one of his customers) while keeping vigilant watch that no one violated Vineland's dry law and trying to persuade the neighboring towns of Millville and Bridgeton to follow suit. Both cities eventually did become dry, but in Bridgeton it came only after three days of rioting and the arrest of all the town's saloonkeepers.

Although Thomas's son Charles went to dental school, he soon decided he was more interested in taking over his father's grape juice business. Charles began an expensive program of advertising and promotion, including sampling of the drink at fairs. Although he decided to change the name from the antiseptic Dr. Welch's Unfermented Wine to the simpler and more friendly Welch's Grape Juice, some ads still stressed the medical angle, touting Welch's as the cure for "typhoid fever, pneumonia, pleuritus...and all forms of chronic disease except diabetes mellitus"—a natural exception given the amount of sugar in grapes. Other ads contained puzzles or games, one offering $10 to the person who could form the largest number of words from the phrase "Welch's Grape Juice." (The winner found 1,366.) Charles appealed to the prohibitionists with an ad featuring a pretty girl and the slogan "The lips that touch Welch's are all that touch mine."

Although Charles's teetotaler father didn't live to see the day, Welch's benefited greatly from the passage of Prohibition in 1919. Actions by several prominent members of the Wilson administration helped. Secretary of State William Jennings Bryan decided to serve Welch's Grape Juice instead of wine at a diplomatic dinner, and Secretary of the Navy Josephus Daniels ordered Welch's Grape Juice substituted for U.S. sailors' monthly ration of rum.

Both politicians were widely ridiculed. One newspaper cartoon showing Uncle Sam drinking grape juice was captioned "Grape Juice Diplomacy." "Give 'em grape, Josephus" became a popular saying. Negative though it may have been, the furor brought attention—and new customers—to Welch's.

Charles Welch died in 1926, only three years after the company began making grape jelly. In subsequent years, Welch's Grape Jelly became as prized for its decorated tumblers as for its delicious pairing with peanut butter. Between 1953 and 1990, four sets of cartoon characters

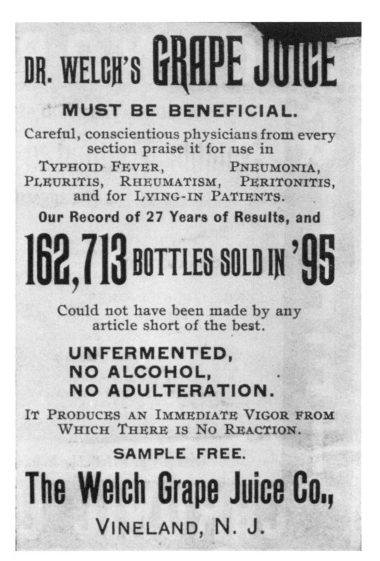

Claims on early ads for Welch's Grape Juice exploited its inventor's medical background and made no secret of his antipathy towards alcohol.

(the Flintstones, Archie, Looney Tunes and Tom & Jerry) and two television shows ("Howdy Doody" and "Davy Crockett") were featured on Welch's glasses.

In 1945, the controlling interest in Welch's was sold to a cooperative of grape growers in New York State. Company headquarters are now located in Concord, Massachusetts, the town where America's native grape was developed. Thomas Welch would undoubtedly be happy to know that most Methodist churches—including his old parish in Vineland, New Jersey—today serve grape juice at communion instead of wine.

KOOL-AID: MAKING A KOOL FORTUNE ON PINT-SIZED THIRST

If you didn't do it yourself, you probably had a friend who set up a Kool-Aid stand in his front yard on hot August afternoons, drinking up most of the stock as he waited for customers or talked to kids too cheap to buy.

From 1930 through the 1960s, these paradigms of pint-sized entrepreneurship became a symbol of summer and childhood as enduring as hoops and jacks had been in an earlier age—so much so that when Charles Schulz put Lucy Van Pelt at a stand with a sign that read "Psychiatric Advice: 5 cents," everyone got the joke.

Kool-Aid inventor Edwin E. Perkins would certainly have approved, for he was the pint-sized entrepreneur par excellence in Hendley, Nebraska. At age 11, he responded to a magazine advertisement that read, "Be a manufacturer—*Mixer's Guide* tells how—write today," and then took over his mother's kitchen making perfumes, patent medicines and other concoctions. The need for labels for his various products led him to respond to another ad that read, "Start a print shop in your own home—make money." Before he was long out of high school, Perkins was printing calling cards, acting as town postmaster and selling his potions with the help of boy and girl "agents" he captured through his own magazine ads.

In 1918 Perkins had a hit in his tobacco quitters kit. Soldiers who had begun smoking in the trenches were just returning home from World War I, so there was a ready market for Perkins's product, which he called Nix-O-Tine. It consisted of large flat tablets of herbs designed to be swallowed, herbs to be chewed, an herbal laxative and a silver nitrate mouthwash—all so unpleasant that those who could endure it probably didn't want to put anything in their mouths again.

Encouraged by the success of Nix-O-Tine, Perkins moved to Hastings, Nebraska, to be nearer to rail lines and expanded his business to include more than 125 flavorings, spices, toilet preparations, medicines and household products under the Onor-Maid label. Products were sold both by direct mail and by door-to-door salesmen.

Soon one product emerged as the sales leader: a fruit-flavored soft drink concentrate called Fruit Smack. It was introduced about the same time that Coca-Cola was gaining national acceptance, but it was concentrated, so a family could make a pitcherful for just pennies. The only problem was that the glass bottles were heavy and often broke while being transported around the country.

Perkins was familiar with Jell-O and figured his drink also could be reduced to a dry powder. He set a chemist to work, and in 1927 the new dry soda concentrate, now named Kool-Aid (borrowing punctuation and the "aid" from Onor-Maid), debuted in envelopes printed on Perkins's own printing press.

By 1929, Perkins's whole family was helping him to weigh out crystals on scales and pound the envelopes flat with wooden mallets so they would fit into the packing boxes. But they couldn't keep up with demand. In the Depression the product found an eager market in the millions of families who were looking to save money. In 1930, Perkins decided to drop all his other products and move the Kool-Aid business to Chicago, where he would be closer to suppliers and distributors. Despite a price cut from 10 to five cents (or maybe because of it), net sales increased from $383,000 in 1931, the first year in Chicago, to $1.5 million in 1936. General Foods acquired the business in 1953.

General Foods executives came up with the idea of the frosted pitcher with the smiling face (a possible inspiration for the ubiquitous "happy face" of the

1970s?) in 1956. Before that, the envelope featured a glass of Kool-Aid and a dish of Kool-Aid-flavored sherbet. In recent years, the pitcher has sprouted arms and legs so that it's able to do more than just sit there looking happy. On the Kool-Aid Kooler cardboard lunch packages, he's shown lifting weights, shooting basketballs and generally being hyperactive—perhaps from the considerable amount of sugar used to make all but the unsweetened versions.

In response to modern concerns, the amount of sugar in presweetened Kool-Aid was reduced in the 1980s. Although General Foods has not changed the amount of sugar called for on the packages of the unsweetened mix, studies show that many parents are adding less. Unsweetened Kool-Aid sells far better than presweetened, probably because it's cheapest and comes in the most flavors.

The best-selling flavors are cherry, lemonade, grape and tropical punch. (Cherry and grape were also among Fruit Smack's six original flavors.) Even though health-conscious moms and dads may prefer 100 percent fruit juices or lemonade, sales surveys show Kool-Aid is still the favorite soft drink of kids ages four to 12.

GATORADE: THE DRINK OF CHAMPIONS

In an era when people are clamoring to pay $100 for sneakers and $5,000 for machines that will replicate the exercise benefits of riding a one-speed bicycle around the block, is it any wonder that people are spending $1 billion this year on sport drinks that some physicians say are only slightly better than drinking water?

The very first sport drink was invented by a kidney doctor at the University of Florida named Robert Cade. In 1965, the coach of the school's losing football team, the Gators, asked Cade if he could explain why his players became so exhausted during the fourth quarter and if anything could be done about it. Cade analyzed the body liquids lost in sweating and by the beginning of the next football season presented the coach with a lemon-lime-flavored restorative drink he named after the team. By 1967, Gatorade was being used by National Football League teams as well as by racehorses and children suffering from severe diarrhea or vomiting. Soon annual sales were well over $50 million.

In the early 1990s, when the health and exercise craze has reached a peak, a number of other sports drinks have entered the sports drink race, but Gatorade still commands 90 percent of the market. Its considerable profits are split between owner Quaker Oats, the University of Florida and several individuals, including Cade, who make up the Gatorade Trust.

Like water, sport drinks are good for preventing dehydration. The sugars in them help to supply energy. The sodium and potassium help to replace electrolytes lost by those who participate in endurance activities such as triathlons. Most nutritionists say these extra ingredients are unnecessary for the casual athlete. In these cases, the main advantage of sports drinks like Gatorade is that their taste tends to get people to drink more than they would if they were just drinking water.

Dr. Cade has used the money he's made from Gatorade to put five students through college, give needy families in his church Studebakers (Cade collects and restores them as a hobby) and fund his own research, including a controversial new treatment for schizophrenia using dialysis, a hydraulic football helmet and a new sports drink (as yet unreleased) that he says is even better than Gatorade.

10

CANDY

CHARITY BEGINS BY EATING A HERSHEY'S CHOCOLATE BAR

In recent years candy bars have become a popular fund-raising tool for schools. What a lot of people probably don't realize is that every time you buy a Hershey's candy bar, you're also supporting a school. It's a school for disadvantaged kids that Milton Hershey founded well before this kind of charitable involvement became politically correct. The school still owns 42 percent of Hershey's common stock.

Milton Hershey's charitable impulses can at least partly be explained by his Mennonite faith and an impoverished childhood that forced him to quit school and begin working full time when he was 15. By the time Hershey was 30 years old, he had almost 15 years of experience in the candy-making business, but he had yet to have a success. When he returned to his hometown of Lancaster, Pennsylvania, in 1886, still owing money to a string of candy suppliers, he was shunned as an irresponsible drifter by most of his relatives.

But Hershey had picked up at least one good idea from his experience making candy: Fresh milk could dramatically improve the flavor of caramel. With a loan from one relative who still believed in him, he began making caramels and selling them from a basket he carried over his arm. By chance, an English importer got a taste of one of Hershey's caramels and gave him a big order. By 1894, Hershey's candy caramel company was doing a booming business. Four years later, after working long hours and living in drab houses by himself that entire time, Hershey, 41, married. The townspeople were shocked. But they were more so when in 1900 he sold his caramel business—and got $1 million.

At this point, many people would retire and spend their lives traveling. But Hershey had seen some chocolate-making equipment at the Chicago Exposition of 1893 that made him want to start all over.

At that time chocolate candy was a delicacy—expensive, not widely available and sold only in individual candy-box pieces. Hershey had the idea that a simple chocolate bar could also be sold successfully in large quantities at a lower price. Instead of the tiny print featured on most food packaging of the day, his chocolate would feature "Hershey's" in huge letters—and thus be its own advertisement everywhere he placed it. And he planned to place it everywhere—at drugstores, coffee counters and grocers.

The idea of mass production would later be used successfully by Henry Ford in making cars. But it first proved itself with candy bars. After building a factory in the town of Derry Church, Pennsylvania (chosen because it was his birthplace and also because it was close to many dairy farms), Hershey began producing the first Hershey's Milk Chocolate Bars® for retail sale around 1905. Hershey's Kisses Milk Chocolates® followed in 1907 (the name came from the puckering noise created when the candy machines deposited the chocolates on a moving belt). By 1911, his company was doing $5 million per year in sales—without advertising.

But Hershey never kept the money all to himself. In addition to giving all his stock in the company to the Milton Hershey School in 1918, Hershey built homes, stores, a bank, a water and electric company and a trolley system—so completely transforming Derry Church that it was renamed Hershey. During the Depression, he kept people in town employed building a luxury hotel, rose gardens, a museum, a sports arena and five golf courses. Today the streetlights in town are shaped like Hershey's Kisses Milk Chocolates, there are avenues named Chocolate and Cocoa and thousands come annually to visit the company's Chocolate World® visitor's center and adjacent amusement park. Choco-

Milton S. Hershey holding one of the boys from the school he founded for orphans. Since the Milton Hershey School owns 42 percent of Hershey's common stock, buying a Hershey's candy bar can in some ways be viewed as a charitable act.

late World, 300 Park Blvd. (800-437-7439), features a 12-minute ride through a mock plant and a gift shop.

Although the company has diversified in recent years, most of Hershey Foods' business still involves chocolate. Producing the Hershey's Milk Chocolate Bar with Almonds has made the company the largest single user of almonds in the United States. Every day Hershey's uses as much milk in its milk chocolate as is used by all the people in a city the size of Philadelphia.

Hershey's placed its first advertisement in 1970, one year after the company raised the price of the Hershey bar from five to 10 cents (the first price increase in 48 years). Hershey Foods continues Milton's commitment to community involvement, giving $50 million to start the medical school at Penn State University, for example. Had he been alive, Milton Hershey would no doubt have been extremely pleased to know that one recent chief executive officer of the company, William E. Dearden, got his start at the Milton Hershey School.

WILL THE REAL BABY RUTH PLEASE STAND UP?

A lot of people think the Baby Ruth candy bar was named after baseball star Babe Ruth. It was actually named for the eldest daughter of President Grover Cleveland, who was born between Cleveland's first and second terms of office and so was regarded as America's "Baby." The whole country mourned when she died in 1904 at age 12.

Curtiss Candy Company owner Otto Schnering originally introduced the peanut, caramel and chocolate-covered candy bar we now know as Baby Ruth in 1920 under the name Kandy Kake, but it was renamed in a company contest a year later. By 1926, Schnering was selling $5 million of the candy bars per day. This wasn't just because of the association with a popular public figure but also because Schnering was a master promoter. Among his most impressive gimmicks was hiring airplanes to drop bars suspended by tiny parachutes over Pittsburgh, convincing Admiral Byrd to carry thousands of Baby Ruths on his famous expedition to the South Pole and getting Dr. Allan Roy Dafoe, doctor to the famous Dionne quintuplets, to endorse the bars as being "rich in Dextrose, vital food-energy sugar." Imagine a food product being advertised like that today!

But Baby Ruth was a well-established brand name before then—so much so that when the New York Yankee named Ruth came out with Babe Ruth's Home Run candy in 1930, the Curtiss Company was able to legally stop him from using his own name.

THE COLORFUL WORLD OF M&M'S

Ouija boards and Magic 8 balls are superstitious products of another age. These days people attribute magical properties to their M&M's.

Although the M&M/Mars company says the candy coatings are unflavored, many people insist that red M&M's taste best. So when the government declared red dye no. 2 a possible carcinogen in 1976 and red M&M's were removed from the mix (not because they contained that dye but because M&M/Mars was afraid people would *think* they did), letters of protest poured into the company, including many from mothers who used them to help teach kids about stoplights. A group of distressed red-M&M fans even formed the Society for the Preservation of Red M&M's. Red came back, without fanfare, in 1987.

Other people believe green M&M's are an aphrodisiac. This rumor has inspired T-shirts that read, "Green M&M's Make You Horny" and a University of Texas sorority house tradition of keeping a large jar filled with green M&M's for "special occasions."

M&M/Mars does extensive consumer research to determine the M&M colors most people like best. Believe it or not, it's different for regular M&M's and M&M peanuts (a variety that is favored by adults and people in the South). The percentages are 30 percent brown, 20 percent yellow and red and 10 percent orange for both plain and peanut, but a package of peanut M&M's contains 20 percent green and no tan rather than the plain's 10 percent green and tan. M&M/Mars spokesman Hans Fiuzzynski can't explain M&M peanut eaters' prejudice against tan, but he thinks people like brown because it tones down the color scheme in the bag. "People tend to prefer a somewhat more subdued appearance for their chocolate assortments," he said.

The rock band Van Halen feels differently. Although they love M&M's, they insist the brown ones be picked out of the bags they order for their dressing rooms.

Things were simpler when M&M's were first created and all of the M&M's were violet colored. M&M's were invented to meet the need for a candy that wouldn't melt in the summer heat in pre-air-conditioned America and subsequently became a popular part of World War II GI rations. That explains the candy's first—and most famous—advertising slogan: "The milk chocolate that melts in your mouth—not in your hand."

That's because some air has been whipped into the milk chocolate to give it someplace to go when it softens. But the colored sugar coating does melt.

Colored hands would seem to be a small price to pay for the experience of crunching into the sugary M&M coating only to discover, a second later, the cushion of chocolate inside. But make sure it's a genuine M&M candy before you pop a few—imitators have a malty taste, and they don't have the telltale M&M insignia outside. (The insignia is printed on each candy by machine in a process similar to offset printing—the same method pill manufacturers use.)

Forrest Mars, son of the inventor of the Milky Way bar and founder of the Mars candy fortune, got the idea for M&M's after becoming acquainted with a similar product called Smarties while living in England. In 1940, he teamed up with another man who grew up with chocolate running through his veins, Bruce Murries—the son of a former Hershey Chocolate Company president.

The M&M name stands for their last names, and for a while, the chocolate centers of the candies contained chocolate from Murries's father's old workplace, Hershey. After M&M merged with Mars in 1964, Hershey and M&M/Mars became archrivals.

In 1991, M&M/Mars introduced a new M&M with a

chocolate and peanut butter filling—the first new flavor of M&M's since peanut came out in 1954. Although they might not be aware of it, even those eating plain M&M's are eating peanuts, for the chocolate in all three flavors of M&M's contains finely ground peanuts—for added flavor.

REESE'S PIECES: A TASTE FROM OUT OF THIS WORLD

How do you catch a creature from another planet? If you're Elliott in the movie *E.T.*, you lure him with a trail of Reese's Pieces®. In one of the film's more dramatic moments, the alien opens up his clenched fist and out drops—not the expected weapon—but brown, yellow and orange pieces of both boy and extraterrestrial's favorite candy.

Those few minutes of screen time sent sales of Reese's Pieces into outer space. Reese's Pieces sales increased 65 percent, causing the company to keep two factories open around the clock. Although the Reese's name is now owned by Hershey's, the products' namesake and inventor of the first and still most popular peanut butter candy, Reese's Peanut Butter Cups®, was a former Hershey employee turned competitor.

Harry "H. B." Reese had worked in a number of different jobs—none of which he found entirely satisfactory—when he moved to Hershey, Pennsylvania, in 1917 to manage one of candy maker Milton Hershey's dairy farms. Inspired by his employer's success and the pressing need to feed and clothe his six children, Reese decided to start his own candy company. Until he took up a customer's suggestion to blend the salty, fatty peanut butter with sweet and smooth milk chocolate (purchased from his old boss Hershey) in 1923, Reese's most successful product was a molasses and coconut candy called Lizzie bars.

For a decade, Reese sold the so-called peanut butter cups only in five-pound boxes for use in candy assortments. (This is why they're still wrapped in candy-box-like brown accordion paper.) But it was only when he introduced them for individual sale that their popularity began to take off.

By the end of World War II, Reese had discontinued all other candies to concentrate on peanut butter cups. The spin-off products were introduced after Hershey's bought the company in 1963, seven years after Reese died. They include Reese's Crunchy Peanut Butter Cups, in 1976; Reese's Peanut Butter Flavored Baking Chips®, in 1977; and Reese's Pieces in 1978.

Film product placements like Reese's Pieces in *E.T.* came under attack by consumer groups in the late 1980s as a new form of subliminal advertising. And they are expensive for companies: Hershey's agreed to spend $1 million on a joint promotion with the movie company after the makers of the movie's first choice, M&M's, turned them down. Since *E.T.*, however, there can at least be no doubt that product placements "phone home" sales.

SUGAR DADDY: ITS INVENTOR IS NO SUCKER FOR COMMUNISTS

If you ever bought a Sugar Daddy lollipop before 1958, there's a chance you helped support the fight against the Communist threat in America. For in 1958, the inventor and maker of that candy went on to found the John Birch Society.

In early life, Robert Welch was a candy hawker on the streets of Cambridge, Massachusetts. At first he only sold candy—three pieces for 10 cents—but eventually he also began making the candy with his brother, James. By 1925 the brothers parted ways—James to make a chocolate-covered fudge bar called Welch's Fudge in a building that he shared with a man named Edwin Land (he had a crazy idea about a plastic film he called Polaroid) and Robert to create a new caramel candy that was 22 percent cream.

Taking his cue from the success of the lollipop, Robert inserted a stick in the caramel slabs and dubbed his creation the Papa Sucker because, he said, it was the biggest and longest lasting, or "Papa" of all lollipops. After an attempt at producing the candy in a Chicago plant proved unprofitable, Robert opened a new plant in Brooklyn, New York, and entered an unusual arrangement with the Brach Candy Company wherein Papa Suckers were made both by Brach in Chicago and independently by Robert in Brooklyn. Robert kept an eye on things by commuting by plane between the two cities every other week.

Just before quitting both jobs in 1932, Robert renamed his candy Sugar Daddy after the then popular expression (referring, as it does now, to a benevo-

lent older man), hoping to get across the idea that his candy offered a wealth of sweetness. Not long afterward, Robert rejoined his brother in Cambridge, taking charge of sales and advertising for Sugar Daddy, the newly invented spin-off Sugar Babies, Welch's Junior Mints, Pom Poms and all of James's many candy products. One of Robert's most successful promotional ideas was to package comic cards (similar to baseball cards but featuring comic characters) inside every Sugar Daddy wrapper in the early 1940s. Kids could get prizes for sending in the comic cards, but avid collectors (including King Farouk of Egypt) saved and traded them instead.

Nabisco bought the James O. Welch Company in 1963 but continued Robert's tradition of great promotions when it gave the Broadway producers of the musical *Sugar Babies* samples of the candy of the same name. Stars Mickey Rooney and Ann Miller threw them into the audience during the performance. Perhaps the greatest public relations boost Sugar Daddy ever enjoyed was from the Bobby Riggs–Billie Jean King tennis Battle of the Sexes at the Houston Astrodome in September 1973. Playing the role of Sugar Daddy with obvious pleasure, Riggs arrived courtside in a rickshaw drawn by a team of young ladies called "Bobby's Bosom Buddies" and presented King with a huge Sugar Daddy sucker—the implication being that she was a sucker to think any woman could beat any man at tennis. (As it turned out, King blasted Riggs off the court, 6–4, 6–3, 6–3.)

This all must have seemed pretty frivolous to Robert Welch, who had by the 1950s left the candy business to form the John Birch Society, a political group named for an Army intelligence officer killed by Chinese Communists just after World War II. Birch was, Welch believed, the first casualty of the Cold War. In the 1950s, the group denounced President Eisenhower as a communist agent and came out against the fluoridation of water as another sign of creeping big government. (Welch apparently no longer cared about the possible positive implications for the candy industry—that maybe with fluoridation, mothers would worry less about their kids eating candy.) Other Birch Society targets have included the civil rights movement, the United Nations, Earth Day and former Supreme Court Chief Justice Earl Warren.

Welch stepped down as head of the Birch Society in 1983, but despite the end of the Cold War, the group still worries about the possibility that the new world order of friendly nations President Bush sometimes talked about was really a conspiracy to form a world socialist government.

Whatever happens, it's likely that between the Birchers' activities and Sugar Daddy sales, Robert Welch's influence, like his caramel lolly, will last a long time.

THE AMAZING ELECTRIC KOOL-AID LIFE SAVER

Forget about savoring and swallowing. Life Savers' best use is as an excuse to lure people of the opposite sex into dark closets.

Tell them it's an experiment utilizing the simple Life Saver candy. Find a closet, close the door, wait a few minutes until your eyes adjust to the dark. Then pop a few Wint-O-Green Life Savers into your mouth and begin chomping away. If all goes well, your friend will be amazed to see a little blue lightning like display of sparks coming out of your mouth.

Kids the world over call this "sparking" or "the electric Life Saver effect." Physicists know it as one of the more prosaic examples of triboluminescence—a phenomenon where light is emitted when certain substances are rubbed, crushed or broken.

How does it work in the case of Life Savers? When the sugar crystals in Wint-O-Green Life Savers break under the pressure of being chewed, positive and negative electric charges separate. Voltage builds up until electrons leap across the fracture, causing nitrogen molecules in the air to emit a tiny burst of blue-white light. (The same thing happens on a much grander scale when the charge differential between clouds and the ground is great enough to initiate lightning, which is why the Life Saver effect is also sometimes called "mouth lightning.")

All this happens in the invisible, ultraviolet region of the light spectrum, which would make it impossible to see if not for the presence of the wintergreen molecules—which glow when excited by the flash of lightning.

The explanation comes from Linda Sweeting, a chemistry professor at Towson State University in Maryland who studied the Wint-O-Green Life Saver a few years back. The principle of triboluminescence was first reported by Sir Francis Bacon in 1605 and was first noticed in Life Savers some years after their invention in 1912.

They were the creation of Clarence Crane (the father of writer Hart Crane), a chocolatier who was looking for a nonperishable candy product to sell during the hot summer months when his regular business usually slacked off. He came up with the idea of a mint shaped in a circle—to distinguish it from the pillow-shaped European mints already on the market. Because of the candy's resemblance to a life preserver, Crane called them Life Savers and ran ads featuring rescues at sea, using the slogan "For That Stormy Breath."

While Clarence Crane launched Life Savers, ad man

Edward John Noble was responsible for its success. After buying the mints in a New York store, Noble promptly struck out for Cleveland to sell streetcar ads to Crane. Crane didn't want to buy an ad but agreed to sell the business to the interested Noble for $2,900.

Almost immediately, Noble ran into a major problem. The cardboard tubes Crane had been packaging the candy in didn't preserve the peppermint flavor— and actually added an off taste of their own. Noble promptly devised a tinfoil shrink-wrap (a first in the industry) and exchanged retailers' tasteless old stock for the new improved one—a move that made him no profit and sent him scrambling for a way to make more money from the candy.

Noble found it by approaching saloon owners, barbers, restaurateurs and other nonfood businesses about carrying Life Savers, encouraging them all to place the candies near the cash register to stimulate impulse buying. "Make sure every customer gets a nickel with his change and see what happens," Noble is supposed to have told them.

Thus Noble can be seen as indirectly responsible for the eventual creation and success of "impulse items" such as Bic lighters, Gillette razor blades, Globe Mini-Books ("How to Lose Weight in Seven Days," "Your Astrological Signs," etc.) and such bastions of American journalism as *TV Guide*, the *National Enquirer* and the *Weekly World News*. The success of Life Savers enabled Noble to buy ABC-TV in 1943 for $8 million in cash.

Today Life Savers are enjoyed by millions of Americans who are too old for lollipops and too young or unself-conscious to buy more medicinally potent breath mints. In fact, 90 percent of all Americans have tried the candy at one time or another. There is even a world's record for keeping a Life Saver in the mouth with the hole intact: 7 hours, 10 minutes, set by Thomas Syta of Van Nuys, California.

Following the success of the tiny Tic Tac breath mints in the 1980s, Life Savers introduced Life Saver Holes in late 1990. Despite the name, these were an entirely new product. Life Savers are made in doughnut-like molds or formed like a rope around a rod, with no candy ever being thrown out.

DOUBLE GOOD WRIGLEY'S GUM

Given the number of kids who've gotten in trouble for chewing gum in school, it's interesting to learn that the creator of America's best-selling gums, William Wrigley, Jr., spent almost as much time in the principal's office as in the classroom. In fact, his biographers estimate that Wrigley's pranks (including hurling a pie at the school's brass nameplate) got him expelled on average once every three weeks until his soap manufacturer father put him to work selling his product.

Wrigley was a tenacious salesman (once sleeping on the doorstep of an elusive wholesaler in order to catch him before he left for work in the morning) who was quick to react to his customers' wants. When, for example, he graduated to his own job as a manufacturers' representative in Chicago in 1891 and discovered that the baking powder boxes he was giving away as a premium to sell his father's soap were more popular than the soap, he added a line of baking powder. When the chewing gum he began giving away as a premium for the baking powder became popular, he decided to concentrate all his energies on selling chewing gum.

In 1893, Wrigley introduced a gum and named it spearmint after the shape of the mint's flower. By 1910, it was the nation's best selling, largely due to Wrigley's advertising and promotional genius. Store owners who

About 1915, William Wrigley, Jr. began using a spear-shaped creature to promote his spearmint gum. Note the ad's reference to the gum's tension-relieving qualities: in fact, chewing gum sales rose during and after both World Wars.

carried his products received a steady supply of useful premiums, including scales, cheese cutters and cash registers. In 1915, all 1.5 million people listed in the nation's phone books received free sticks of Wrigley gum in the mail. In addition, Wrigley spent more money on advertising a single product than ever before.

In the 1910s, 1920s and 1930s, ads for Wrigley's Spearmint Gum featured a spear-shaped creature (by the 1960s, he looked more like a little boy with a stick of gum for a body). In 1939, the company began the tradition of using a pair of attractive twin women to represent Doublemint Gum. In total, about five sets of women twins and one set of men were featured up until the 1980s. In the early 1990s, Wrigley's ad agency switched to quick vignettes of many sets of twins doing fun things replayed over the course of a 15-second commercial—in effect, doubling the doubles.

Doublemint Gum was introduced in 1914. After that, the company didn't introduce a new product for 59 years. For most of those years, Wrigley gums sold best. That's where William Wrigley got the money to buy Catalina Island, and an interest in the Chicago Cubs and to build Chicago's famous Wrigley Building.

Unlike many other businesses, Wrigley's has always done the best during bad economic times. Psychologists say this is because chewing gum is a great tension and irritation reliever. Wrigley himself once said, "People chew harder when they're sad."

THE RUMOR OF HIS DEATH BY POP ROCKS WAS GREATLY EXAGGERATED

In 1978, children in most playgrounds in America could have told you how the little boy who played Mikey on the Life cereal commercial had died from eating Pop Rocks and drinking Coca-Cola at the same time.

It wasn't true. John Gilchrist is alive and well and still hating everything. And Pop Rocks are a harmless confection containing only one tenth of the carbonation of a 12-ounce can of soda. The only unexpected consequence of eating them is usually a broad grin or laughter.

"Rumor!" author Hal Morgan called it a classic example of a childhood bravery story—spread by children who were so excited by the fizzy, poppy candy that they decided to add an element of danger to it too. The Food and Drug Administration set up a Pop Rocks hot line in one city to allay parents' fears about the product. Fortunately for General Foods, it failed to end the Pop Rocks Phenomenon, the name given to explain the hundreds of millions of packages of the stuff that were sold in the late 1970s.

Pop Rocks were invented unintentionally in 1956 by William Mitchell, a chemist for General Foods. Mitchell was really trying to create a powdered carbonated soda.

Mitchell introduced carbon dioxide into candy while it was still a liquid, trapping the gas into tiny candy pockets when it cooled. To his dismay, he found that the carbonation wouldn't last more than a few minutes when the dry pellets were put in water. But they did produce a curious, smile-producing sensation in the mouth when exposed to the moisture there—an effect that his friends in the lab and kids all enjoyed.

General Foods waited almost 20 years before deciding to market the product as a candy and discontinued production in the 1980s. A smaller company reintroduced Pop Rocks in 1987, the same year that a teenage John Gilchrist was featured in a new Life cereal commercial.

11

CONDIMENTS

THE ISLAND PRESERVE OF THE TABASCO PEPPER

Among those who rate the quality of their food by how much it makes their nose run and tongue sting, McIlhenny Company's Tabasco® brand pepper sauce is a culinary WD-40. A squirt or two of it can fix anything.

But environmentalists and birders revere the McIlhenny Company for another reason. In the late 19th century, on the grounds of the property where Tabasco pepper sauce is made, E. A. McIlhenny helped save the snowy egret from extinction and created a sanctuary for birds so big it is known as Bird City. He also helped work for national legislation that protected migratory water birds and waterfowl.

Tabasco sauce was created by E. A.'s father, Edmund McIlhenny, a New Orleans banker who married Mary Eliza Avery in 1859. Avery was the eldest daughter of a family who owned and operated a salt mine on the 2,300-acre Avery Island in the bayou country of southern Louisiana. Because salt was vital in preserving meat for troops during the Civil War, the Union Army captured Avery Island early in the war. The McIlhennys and Averys took refuge in Texas during the war. When they returned, all was in shambles except a crop of especially flavorful Mexican hot peppers Edmund had planted from seeds a friend had given him.

Among the many dishes McIlhenny made with the peppers was a spicy sauce of chopped red peppers and native Avery Island salt, aged in wooden barrels, then mixed with vinegar. He called the sauce Tabasco after a Mexican word of Indian origin.

Encouraged by the enthusiasm of friends who had tried it, McIlhenny began bottling the sauce in old cologne bottles (the model for the bottle used today) and sending it off to Southern wholesalers. By late 1870, the sauce was so popular (especially for use in seafood dishes) that he was able to open an international office in London.

Edmund died in 1890, but the Tabasco sauce legacy was continued by a string of colorful McIlhenny family members, including Edmund's son E. A., a naturalist who went to the Arctic with Admiral Perry and later organized his own Alaskan expedition to study migratory birds. When E. A. returned to Avery Island in 1892 and found that hunting was dramatically depleting the exotic bird population on the island, he built a large cage over a pond where the few remaining snowy egrets could mate and make nests. As the bird population began to build back up, E. A. built a landing platform over the pond and imported exotic plants and animals. In the midst of all this natural splendor is a Buddha that was created during the reign of Emperor Hui-Tsung and given to E. A. in 1937 by friends who lived in New York City.

Another one of Edmund's sons, John Avery McIlhenny, had been a member of Teddy Roosevelt's Rough Riders and often visited the Roosevelts at the White House. When the president's daughter, Alice, visited Avery Island, a big dinner was staged in her honor at the salt mine. Current company president Ned Simmons said, "The tables and chairs were carved out of salt, and candelabra filled the mine with light while servants stood in the shadows, singing. All the men wore white tie, of course."

E. A.'s nephew, Walter, was just as colorful in his own way. A retired brigadier general in the U.S. Marine Corps, he was a big-game hunter and crack marksman who also enjoyed fine cooking and wines. Walter's two interests came together during the Vietnam War, when he hired a chef and a mess sergeant to formulate some gourmet meals that could be produced in the field from ordinary C-rations. The resulting "Charlie Ration Cookbook" went out to thousands of soldiers wrapped around a two-ounce bottle of Tabasco pepper sauce in a special waterproof canister.

The company is still family owned and operated (President Simmons is the founder's great-grandson), and though most of the peppers used are grown in Mexico, Colombia and Honduras, Avery Island is the source of most of the pepper seeds. After harvesting, these are stored in a bank vault until the next planting season. Although Walter tried to figure out how to speed up the Tabasco-making process, the resulting sauce didn't taste as good. So the pepper-salt mash is still aged in wooden barrels for three years, just as it has always been.

Despite the old joke about there being no such thing as an empty Tabasco bottle, the company sells more than 75 million two-ounce bottles of the sauce each year in America alone. The Tabasco company tour and surrounding gardens and bird sanctuary also make Avery Island a major tourist attraction. The Tabasco pepper sauce factory visitor's center (318-365-8173) is visited by 100,000 people each year.

LEA & PERRINS: A NOBLE SAUCE

The story of Lea & Perrins Worcestershire sauce is almost all there on its tan wrapper and orange label.

The statement "From a recipe of a nobleman in the country" on the label refers to Sir Marcus Sandys, a nobleman from Worcester, England, who became fond of a certain popular seasoning sauce while on assignment as governor of the province of Bengal, India. When he came back to his native land, Sandys gave a recipe for the sauce to Lea & Perrins, a Worcester chemist shop run by John Lea and William Perrins, and asked them to make up a batch for himself and some of his friends. But when Sandys tried what they came up with, it tasted nothing like the sauce he had known and loved in India.

Lea & Perrins put the failed brew into their basement, where it sat until someone got the idea to give it another try. After aging, it was delicious.

Lea & Perrin's secured Sandys's permission to sell the sauce to the public, and it was so popular that they soon had many competitors. That's why the label reads, "The Original and Genuine Worcestershire Sauce." The label also lists as ingredients "water, vinegar, molasses, corn sweeteners, anchovies (and/or sardines), natural flavorings, onions, tamarinds, salt, garlic, cloves, chili peppers and eschalots." Because all this stuff sits around in vats of vinegar for two years, it also probably contains dissolved anchovy bones.

HENRY HEINZ PASSED OUT A PECK OF PICKLE PINS (AMONG OTHER PROMOTIONS)

If you visited Atlantic City before 1944, went to the World's Fair in 1965 or 1982, or traveled through Pittsburgh sometime before 1972, chances are you have a little plastic pickle pin stashed away in a jewelry box or drawer. For years they were what the pickle-producing H. J. Heinz company handed out to visitors at its Atlantic City pavilion, World's Fair booths and Pittsburgh plant. At the end of the 19th century, it became all the rage for schoolchildren to wear the little pins on their shirt lapels, sweaters, blouses and caps. Adults who didn't wear them still found them hard to throw away.

Henry J. Heinz started distributing the one-and-a-half-inch gutta-percha pickles in the form of watch charms at the 1893 Chicago World's Fair. Having been assigned an out-of-the-way booth, Heinz decided to drum up business by distributing coupons promising a free gift to any fairgoer who visited the Heinz exhibit. So many people took Heinz up on the offer that workmen had to be brought in to reinforce the girders under Heinz's part of the exhibition floor.

At the time of the pickle promotion, Heinz was trying to make a go of his second condiment company. In 1869 he formed a company with L. C. Noble to make

100 percent horseradish in clear glass jars (competitors hid the fact that theirs was half turnip greens behind green glass). But that company went under in the financial panic of 1875. When Heinz took another stab at it in 1876, he was more conservative with growth and more flamboyant about promotion.

For instance, the state-of-the-art factory complex he built on the Allegheny River in 1888 included such extras as a Turkish bath for horses with colds and a glass tank containing an 800-pound, 14½-foot, (supposedly) 150-year-old live alligator he had acquired on a trip to Florida that helped to make the Heinz buildings a must-see for anyone visiting Pittsburgh. In 1899, he built another tourist attraction on the pier at Atlantic City. The Heinz Pier featured, among other things, free restrooms, souvenir cards and stationery; free samples of Heinz products; free admission to a gallery of some 144 paintings, bronzes, tapestries and curios Heinz had picked up in his travels; and, of course, free pickle pins.

In 1900, Heinz also erected one of New York's first large electric signs (at Fifth Avenue and 23rd Street). It featured a 40-foot-long pickle, and 1,200 light bulbs and cost $90 to light each night.

Heinz was also behind the keystone shape and "57 varieties" slogan of Heinz labels today. The keystone was probably the result of Heinz's early involvement with Keystone Pickling & Preserving Works or possibly was chosen because the keystone is the Pennsylvania state symbol. He was inspired to create the "57 varieties" when the trolley car he was riding in passed a sign for a shoe store that advertised "21 styles" of shoes. His company was actually making more than 60 products at the time, but he thought that 57 sounded better.

Although Heinz and its Weight Watchers, Star–Kist and Ore–Ida affiliates today produce more than 3,000 food products worldwide, the number 57 remains on the labels, as the last two digits of corporate headquarters' phone number and the name of its popular steak sauce. And the company still gives out pickle pins at supermarket conventions and, as recently as 1990, through the mail in connection with a National Public Radio broadcast of a Heinz Foundation–sponsored Pittsburgh Symphony concert.

HEINZ: THE SLO-O-O-W KETCHUP

Have you ever parked a bottle of ketchup over your food, started whacking on the bottom and had someone else at the table (usually the chef) groan, "Don't do that! You're going to ruin it!" If what you've got on your plate is gourmet fare of a delicately balanced, delicious sort, they may have a point.

But the combination of tomatoes, sweetener, onions and spices that is ketchup provides just the zip that many good but slightly dull foods need: foods such as hamburgers, french fries, meat pies, beans and codfish cakes. (And—let's be honest—it's also a great cover-up for foods people just plain don't like.) That's probably why ketchup was long the most popular condiment in America (although salsa has just taken over the number one spot).

Ketchup like toppings have been in use since Roman times, but their life as a commercial product began in 1876 when Henry J. Heinz decided to expand his horseradish company to make it possible for families to enjoy ketchup without having to spend the long hours required to cook it at home. In fact, Heinz

In 1911, workers hand chose tomatoes that were used as an ingredient in Heinz ketchup.

Ketchup was first advertised as "Blessed Relief for Mother and Other Women of the Household."

The ingredients he used are virtually identical to the ones used today but the consistency of this early version was quite thin, so it was packed in a bottle with a narrow neck intended to help impede the flow. The bottle was later made into an octagonal shape to make it easier to grip.

The design of that bottle has changed little in the intervening 110-plus years, even though the ketchup Heinz put in it got thicker. That explains why it is so difficult to get the ketchup out of these bottles today. Research shows that consumers like the thicker ketchup. With the introduction of a 12-ounce wide-mouthed bottle in the 1960s, it seemed they had a bit of a masochistic streak as well, for the wide-mouthed bottle soon became the least popular member of the Heinz Ketchup family. But when Heinz introduced the squeezable plastic bottle in 1983, it became apparent that people did too want an easier way to get the ketchup out more easily—they just didn't want to have to spoon it out. Now more than 60 percent of all Heinz Ketchup is sold in these plastic containers.

The Heinz Ketchup bottle's neckband is also a vestige of an earlier era. In the 1800s, the bottles were sealed with a cork, and the neckband helped to keep a foil cap snug against its cork and sealing wax. Today its main job is to help distinguish Heinz from its competitors.

GREY POUPON MUSTARD: A TASTE OF THE GOOD LIFE

Pardon me," one chauffeur-driven executive asks another as their Rolls-Royces cross paths, "would you have any Grey Poupon?" "But of course," is the reply as one man hands a jar over to the other.

The ads ranked Grey Poupon as "one of life's finest pleasures." Their implied message: You may not be able to afford a Rolls or a yacht, but you can get a taste of the good life by buying a $1.89 jar of Grey Poupon mustard.

The ads worked like a $20 tip—boosting Grey Poupon's sales to second among American mustards in dollars earned and appearing in recipes in women's magazines for such nouvelle cuisine as Dijon chicken and Dijon vinaigrette. They also helped to create a new fad: brides and grooms handing bottles of Grey Poupon out the windows of limousines. Some limousine companies throw in a case of Grey Poupon as a Rolls-Royce rental promotion.

Grey Poupon may have only recently taken mustard out of the ballpark and into the mansions of America, but fine mustard has been made in Dijon, France, since the 13th century. According to one story, the word *mustard* itself comes from a coat of arms the Duke of Burgundy awarded the city of Dijon in recognition of its military achievements. The coat of arms read, *Moult Me Tarde*, or "I Ardently Desire," but the woodcarver forgot the middle word, so the motto instead translated to, "To Burn Much." Travelers thought this so funny they began calling the mustard seed from that city *Moultarde*. Of course, it would also make sense to think people might call a hot and spicy condiment by a name like "burnt much." In any case, Dijon was so famous for its mustard that in 1634 laws were passed to regulate its production, including one requiring those who made it to wear only "clean and modest clothes."

In 1777, the mustard firm that was to become the most famous of all in the city was founded by Monsieur Grey and Monsieur Poupon. Poupon had the money; Grey had a secret recipe for a strong mustard made with white wine that would become the standardbearer of the Dijon variety. In 1850, Grey also invented the first automated mustard machines (operated by steam)—thus greatly improving the lives of workers in his and other mustard factories and earning him two medals of honor from the Dijon Academy of Arts, Sciences and Letters.

Although city laws no longer dictate what a mustard

maker must wear, *"appellation controllee"* standards similar to those used for fine French wines still control the way Dijon mustard is made. For instance, all Dijon must be made of brown or black mustard seeds, then seasoned by the addition of wine or vinegar and various spices and herbs.

Grey Poupon is owned by the all-American Nabisco company and is made in Oxnard, California. But the building where Grey and Poupon started their business still stands at 32 Rue de la Liberté. Every year, it attracts hundreds of mustard lovers like, well—mustard to ham.

Bring Out the Hellmann's and Bring On the Summer

Today mayonnaise is as much a part of summer as bug spray and suntan lotion. Picnic foods from sandwiches to coleslaw to potato salad all have mayonnaise as a primary ingredient. This probably would not be true but for Richard Hellmann, the maker of America's first and favorite commercial mayonnaise.

Mayonnaise was first made in Spain and got its name from the French duke Richelieu, who sampled it in Mahón—the chief city of the Spanish Balearic Island of Minorca. Hence he called it the sauce of Mahón or "mahonnaise."

Before people could buy mayonnaise, they had to beat oil into raw eggs to create a thickened sauce, a difficult task that not only offers the risk of failure but also, when it's eaten, the risk of contracting salmonella from the raw eggs.

Richard Hellman first ladled mayonnaise out of big glass jars decorated with blue ribbons he kept on top of his New York City deli counter. He reproduced the ribbon on the labels of the first jars he sold in grocery stores in 1913.

Richard Hellmann was a German immigrant who opened a deli on Columbus Avenue in New York City that was particularly known for its prepared salads. Attributing the compliments to the mayonnaise used, he decided to begin selling it separately as a "to go" item. At first, he displayed the mayonnaise on top of the deli counter in two big glass jars decorated by blue ribbons (a precursor of the blue ribbon printed on Hellmann's labels today) and ladled portions out to be weighed on wooden boats. Later he sold it in individual glass jars. By 1915, manufacturing mayonnaise had become Hellmann's only business.

In 1937, the wife of company sales distributor Paul Price came up with a recipe for a dense, brownielike cake using mayonnaise as a main ingredient. It was to become a favorite of millions. The mayonnaise replaces the shortening traditionally used in cake recipes without actually revealing its own flavor. Hellmann's is more typically used to make sandwiches and salads, which is why sales are best between Memorial Day and Labor Day and actually peak right around the Fourth of July.

Chocolate Mayonnaise Cake

2 cups unsifted flour (or 2¼ cups unsifted cake flour)
⅔ cup unsweetened cocoa
1¼ teaspoons baking soda
¼ teaspoon baking powder
3 eggs
1⅔ cups sugar
1 teaspoon vanilla
1 cup real mayonnaise
1⅓ cups water

Grease and flour bottoms of two 9 × 1½-inch round cake pans. In medium bowl stir flour, cocoa, baking soda and baking powder; set aside. In large bowl with mixer at high speed, beat eggs, sugar and vanilla, scraping bowl occasionally, 3 minutes or until light and fluffy. Reduce speed to low; beat in real mayonnaise until blended. Add flour mixture in 4 additions alternately with water, beginning and ending with flour. Pour into prepared pans. Bake in 350 degree oven 30 to 35 minutes or until cake tester inserted in center comes out clean. Cool in pans on wire racks 10 minutes. Remove; cool completely on racks. Frost as desired. Makes one 9-inch layer cake.

LOG CABIN: SWEET MEMORIES OF AN OLD TIN CAN

Today almost all maple syrups sold in the supermarket come in plastic bottles. The only way to distinguish Log Cabin from Aunt Jemima or Vermont Maid is by reading the name on the label and seeing if the picture is of a woman or a rustic cabin. Not so long ago, though, Log Cabin was distinguished by the log-cabin-shaped tin it came in. Ask anyone over age 60 and they'll probably drift into sweet memories of the tins sitting on the table at Sunday morning breakfast and how, when the syrup had been finished, they would rinse the tins out and use them to play with.

But packaging was not the only unique thing about Log Cabin: when it was introduced in 1887, it was also the first syrup blend to include maple flavor.

In the mid-1800s, what passed as pancake syrup in most households was a corn or molasses and sugarcane blend that was ladled out of huge barrels at the neighborhood store. P. J. Towle of Chicago was one grocer who wasn't satisfied with the taste of the product or the unsanitary way it was sold. Towle knew that maple syrup tasted better, but because of the number of forests that had been cut to settle America, it was in short supply and very expensive. So Towle created a blend of maple syrup and the less expensive sugarcane kind.

Towle called it Log Cabin because a log cabin had been the birthplace of his boyhood hero, Abraham Lincoln. He already had decided he wanted to put the syrup in sealed containers to improve on the hygiene of open barrels. Why not make the containers in the shape of log cabins?

Early examples of these tins read, "Towle Maple Syrup Co., Fairfax, Vt., and St. Paul, Minn." Since Towle had his only factory in St. Paul, Fairfax was probably where he got his maple syrup. To emphasize the superior hygienics of individual packaging, the label also bore a Certificate of Purity that promised a $500 reward to anybody who could find evidence of contamination.

Although his product sold well, Log Cabin didn't become a bestseller until 1918, six years after Towle died. During that era top Log Cabin salesmen were earning bonuses of $50,000 and a full trainload of the syrup moved out of the St. Paul factory each week. In 1927, Towle's sons sold the business to General Foods, which kept making the tin containers, with minor changes in style, until metal shortages during World War II forced a change to glass. One of the most interesting designs, introduced in the 1930s and prized by collectors, features cartoons of girls, boys, dogs, bears, owls and rabbits praising the syrup. In one panel, a boy eating pancakes inside the cabin shouts out the window to his dog, "I'll save one for you, Fido!" and the dog replies, "Don't forget the Log Cabin syrup!"

Today 99 percent of the breakfast syrup sold in America is of the blended type that Towle introduced. But the only maple syrups sold in log cabin tins are gourmet brands containing 100 percent pure maple syrup.

12
DAIRY

ROLLING IN THE DOUGH(BOY) AT PILLSBURY

Pillsbury Crescent dinner rolls and Hungry Jack biscuits may taste good, but what makes them special is the way they're packaged and dispensed: in cardboard tubes that literally burst forth with dough upon opening.

Rudy Perz, an employee of the Leo Burnett Advertising Agency in Chicago, was thinking this very thought as he was trying to come up with an advertising campaign for Pillsbury's refrigerated products in 1965. In place of the dough, he imagined a cute, friendly, pudgy little dough man with a chef's hat popping out of the can. The Pillsbury Doughboy was born.

In his very first commercial, the fantastical creature identified himself as "Poppin' Fresh" and performed a two-step on a kitchen counter. In most ads, he offered helpful hints to homemakers preparing Pillsbury refrigerated biscuits, rolls and cookies. Within a few years of Poppin' Fresh's introduction, more than 87 percent of people surveyed could identify him as a symbol of the Pillsbury Company. More importantly, the Doughboy was responsible for sales of Pillsbury refrigerated products rising to their highest point since Pillsbury had purchased the business from a Southern company called Ballard and Ballard in 1951.

Refrigerated biscuits had been invented 20 years earlier by a Louisville, Kentucky, baker named Lively Willoughby. In the South of the 1930s, flour was newly affordable due to increased supplies from the Midwest, and hot biscuits were a staple of at least one daily meal. Willoughby thought he could expand his local bakery business if he could do most of the work of baking for local homemakers, supplying them with uncooked biscuits that they could store in their ice-boxes for a few hours, then bake.

At first, Willoughby hired boys to deliver pans of the uncooked biscuits door to door on their bicycles—exchanging empty pans for full ones much as milkmen used to pick up glass bottles. Eventually he came up with a method for wrapping the dough in tin foil and putting it in heavy paper cans sealed with metal lids to create a pressurized package that would keep the biscuits fresh in the icebox for a week instead of a day. Consumers had to saw open the cardboard tubes with a knife.

When Pillsbury took over the company Willoughby had sold out to, they redesigned the can into an instrument of kitchen destruction—to open it, you had to give it a good, aggression-relieving whack on the edge of a table or countertop. Food industry insiders called it the "whomp 'em can." In order to avoid lawsuits, Pillsbury switched to a can that could be opened with the gentle prodding of a spoon in 1976. Today consumers can make the Pillsbury Doughboy jump out of the can just by peeling the outside label.

The 1970s and 1980s were not a poppin good time for the Doughboy. Although dolls and cookie jars were made in his likeness, he was upstaged in the ads by human actors. During these years, the Doughboy's only role seemed to be to get his belly poked at the end of commercials. In an era of high technology and feelin'

groovy, the Doughboy seemed square and silly. So silly, in fact, that a Doughboy-like figure (actually identified as the Stay Puft Marshmallow Man) became the instrument of New York City's destruction at the end of the 1984 movie *Ghostbusters*.

But with the return of interest in cooking in the late 1980s came the return of the Doughboy to Pillsbury commercials in a starring role. In keeping with new concerns about health and physical fitness, the Doughboy became almost frenetically active: strumming an air guitar in a spot for cinnamon rolls, playing the concertina for soft breadsticks, and skipping down a stack of books to promote a cookie study break. Different ads showed him playing six different instruments in four different musical styles (including rap and opera).

A recent study of advertising cartoon characters shows the Doughboy to be more popular than Tony the Tiger, Charlie the Tuna or the California Raisins. In an interview promulgated by Pillsbury, Ellen Weis, director of the Museum of Modern Mythology in San Francisco, waxed philosophical about Poppin' Fresh's appeal. "Symbols are visual messages that suggest how we participate. They constantly remind us who we are and how we function in American society. Symbolically, the Pillsbury Doughboy represents home and hearth."

But former Pillsbury baked goods president Michael Paxton has a simpler explanation: People want to poke him in the belly and make him giggle, he said.

PHILADELPHIA BRAND CREAM CHEESE: THE CITY OF HEAVENLY CREAM CHEESE WAS REALLY IN NEW YORK STATE

Philadelphia Brand cream cheese originated in Philadelphia, right? No, it was actually first made in New York State—and was only called Philadelphia to cash in on that city's reputation as the home of fine food products.

Like ice cream and hot dogs, cream cheese is a food native to America. Although his first name has been lost to history, the last name of the dairy owner who first thought to combine cream and milk to make a creamy white cheese was Lawrence. The year was 1872. The new product was quickly popular with both customers and the dairies that began manufacturing it. When a cheese distributor named Reynolds hired Lawrence and another nearby cream cheese maker named Empire to supply him with product, Reynolds adopted Philadelphia Brand as his trademark.

In 1928, Reynolds's successor company merged with Kraft—the company that still makes Philadelphia cream cheese today. In fact, Philadelphia Brand cream cheeses now account for about 10 percent of all Kraft's cheese sales.

In 1947, Kraft began pushing "Philly's" use in cooking during the long cooking demonstration– commercials featured on breaks from the "Kraft Television Theater" TV show. When a recipe for clam appetizer dip first appeared on the show in the late 1940s, eager New York City chefs cleared city grocery stores of canned clams in 24 hours. This was followed by a recipe for an even fancier hot dip using Philly and canned crabmeat.

Philadelphia cream cheese was also the frosting in an exotic sandwich loaf that in looks and construction more closely resembled cake. In the back-to-nature 1960s and 1970s, Philadelphia cream cheese was de rigueur for making carrot cake frosting and cheesecake. In fact, to celebrate the 100th anniversary of the brand in 1981, Kraft held a dinner attended by food giants Jacques Pepin and James Beard that featured a birthday cheesecake measuring six feet long, 30 inches wide, and 14 inches high and containing 774 pounds of Philadelphia Brand cream cheese.

But mostly people eat Philadelphia cream cheese with bagels. In 1984, Kraft got something to spread it on when they bought Lender's Bagels.

Clam Appetizer Dip

1 6½-oz. can minced clams, drained, reserving
 ¼ cup liquid
1 8-oz. package Philadelphia Brand cream cheese, softened
2 teaspoons lemon juice
1½ teaspoons Worcestershire sauce
¼ teaspoon garlic salt
Dash pepper

Mix clams, reserved liquid and remaining ingredients until well blended. Refrigerate. Serve with potato chips or vegetable dippers. Makes 1½ cups.

CHEEZ WHIZ: THE RAREBIT OF PLEBEIANS

Before microwaves, melting cheese over foods usually meant someone had to shred it first. Making a cheese sauce for a fancy vegetable dish was also a delicate process, involving scalding and the ever-present danger of lumpiness. So it's no wonder that cooks in the 1950s went crazy for Cheez Whiz.

In the summer of 1953, Cheez Whiz joined Kraft's large line of products designed to make cheese as friendly, approachable and easy to choose as a loaf of bread. Instead of trying to figure out the difference between Fontina and Brie, the consumer of Kraft cheeses has only to decide whether she wants her cheese sliced, in an aerosol can, in a loaf or, as is the case with Cheez Whiz, as a cheesy sauce in a jar. Kraft's loaf form of processed cheese, Velveeta, had helped pave the way for the acceptance of Cheez Whiz more than 20 years earlier. An extensive series of tests conducted at Rutgers University concluded that processed cheese food such as Velveeta was every bit as digestible and nutritious as milk. To measure "the ability of Velveeta to support muscular work," test subjects were made to ride a stationary bicycle with a huge metal bucket, called a respiration helmet, over their heads.

"Project Cheez Whiz" as it was called in the Kraft company newsletter, "The Kraftsman," began in 1951 and lasted for 18 months. Laboratory men at Kraft originally were aiming at the cheese rarebit trade. Realizing that most Americans didn't even know what rarebit was (never mind want some), Kraft sales and advertising men asked for an all-purpose cheese sauce instead. Many purposes Cheez Whiz certainly could have: in a survey conducted just before the product was released, housewives suggested more than 1,304 uses. Some of the most popular included spooning it over vegetables and casseroles, making macaroni and cheese, and turning hot dogs into cheese dogs and hamburgers into cheeseburgers. In fact, Louis' Lunch in New Haven, Connecticut, an establishment National Public Radio's "All Things Considered" program once identified as making one of the best hamburgers in America (and others claim is the actual birthplace of the hamburger), makes them with freshly ground beef, toasted Pepperidge Farm white bread and Cheez Whiz.

The invention of the microwave has rendered Cheez Whiz less gee-whiz impressive. In a pinch it is now possible to simply nuke some Velveeta into a cheese sauce. But those raised on Cheez Whiz and fans of the product in Puerto Rico (the Cheez Whiz sales capital of the world due largely to the popularity of La Mexda, a dish combining Cheez Whiz, mayonnaise and Spam) would probably not go for this. For them, only that mixture of cheese, water, whey, sodium phosphate, milk fat, skim milk, salt, Worcestershire sauce, mustard flour, lactic and sorbic acid and coloring will do.

Kraft Singles and America's Love Affair with Cheese

Kraft Singles have been part of sandwiches in America for the past 40 years—long enough that the idea of cheese being sanitary, tasty but not too strongly flavored, perfectly pre-sliced and individually wrapped is assumed. That's probably because most moderns have never gotten a whiff of a cheese wheel that's been sitting around in a hot store for a couple of days or watched the exposed ends of the cheese they bought dry out to the point of being inedible.

But as a grocery clerk in Ontario, Canada, James Kraft experienced both. Growing up in a Mennonite farm family, Kraft was plagued by an undiagnosed eye problem that gave him almost daily headaches and by a strict disciplinarian mother who used a thimble on what was left of a finger (cut in a farm machinery accident) to rap her children on the head whenever they did anything wrong. He lived in this environment and clerked in a local grocery store for almost 11 years after high school graduation before escaping to Buffalo to attend business college. When he moved to Chicago to watch over the Midwestern branch of a Buffalo cheese company he had invested in, his bad luck returned, for his partners eased him out. That's when Kraft decided to start his own business delivering cheese to local stores in a horse and buggy.

Remembering the problems with dried-out cheese from his days as a store clerk, Kraft began selling his cheese in small pieces and packaging them in glass jars or wrapped in tinfoil. For the next decade he experi-mented with ways to retard cheese spoilage using nothing more than a 50-cent double boiler and his kitchen stove. In 1916, he got a patent for his method of grinding, blending and pasteurizing cheese into a long-lasting food that could be cut and sold in convenient sizes.

By this time James's four brothers had joined him in business. He needed the help because between 1915, when he invented so-called process cheese, and 1916, company sales went from $5,000 to $150,000. The U.S. government got wind of how well the cheese kept and ordered 6 million tons of it to feed soldiers during World War I.

The war cheese was packaged in tins, but in 1921 Kraft wrapped the five-pound cheese loaves in foil and set them inside rectangular wooden boxes for home consumption. Within a month Kraft had to make 15,000 boxes a day to meet the demand for the cheese. The boxes became hugely popular as storage containers. (It was a lesson in reusable packaging that Kraft General Foods would later exploit in containers used for Cool Whip and Cheez Whiz, to give just two examples.)

Kraft knew that Americans were sandwich freaks, so he made the five-pound loaf the perfect shape for cutting into sandwich-size slices. But when the slices were cut by the grocer, the Kraft cheese lost its brand identity and sometimes some of its freshness. In the 1940s, Kraft experimented with machinery that would slice and wrap cheese in the factory. In 1947, the company decided to test the new product on supermarket shoppers in Detroit, Michigan, in an experiment that "The Kraftsman," Kraft's internal newsletter, solemnly called "the turning point in the story of cheese in slices."

At first, shoppers were skeptical. Under all the packaging, the slices looked so much like a solid block of cheese that housewives didn't believe it was sliced. Salesmen soon found that the best way to sell the product was to open a few sample packages and fan the cheese slices out like a deck of cards. In some stores, the open packages were the only ones shoppers would buy. As a result one Kraft salesman spent practically an entire day opening packages in a grocery store. In 1965, Kraft further wowed consumers when it developed the technology to individually wrap each slice.

No Krafts are now involved in running Kraft USA, a part of Kraft General Foods. James Kraft died in 1953 at age 78. His brother John reportedly was squeezed out of the business by a New York holding company (echoing what happened to James when he first moved to Chicago) and went on to start a company specializing in sesame-seed-based vegetarian products. When the company didn't succeed, John Kraft sold most of his sesame seeds to McDonald's for use on its hamburger buns.

Kraft is still the leading maker of cheese in America, and the company that is credited with increasing the average American's consumption of cheese from less than a pound a year to more than 19 today.

CHURNING OUT BUTTER IN THE LAND O' LAKES

Minnesota's license plates advertise the state as the "Land of 10,000 Lakes," but that's an understatement. The state is actually home to 15,291 lakes of 10 acres or more. It makes sense, then, that Minnesota's largest dairy cooperative and the nation's number-one supplier of butter would be called Land O' Lakes.

Land O' Lakes began in 1921 when 350 dairy farmers got together for their mutual business benefit: mainly to save money on shipping and obtain better prices for their goods. But they went on to accomplish much more. At the time, standards for the production of butter were not particularly high. In fact, most butter sold in the early 1920s was actually made of cream that had gone sour and so had a yogurt or buttermilk-like tang to it. But the farmers in the Land O' Lakes cooperative made only fresh, sweet cream butter and implemented quality control so that any butter below a certain point score could not be sold under the apostrophe-less Land O' Lakes brand name. (The company name, by contrast, uses the punctuation.) The cooperative was also among the first to sell butter in convenient, consumer-size quarters instead of the large, bulky containers then commonly used.

The origins of the Land O' Lakes Indian maiden have been lost to history, but company spokesman Terry Nagle believes she was chosen because of the region's associations with Hiawatha and Minnehaha. The original drawing (which Nagle admits is "a white person's idea of an Indian maiden") showed her shielding the sun with one hand as she looked out over a lake. But in 1928 that changed to the more sedentary, salemanlike pose we see today. The drawing has changed only slightly over the years. However, the company stopped hiring models dressed as the maiden to hawk butter and cheese at trade shows after some Chippewas protested.

The Land O' Lakes brand name was the result of a contest held three years after the cooperative's formation. The governor of Minnesota and the mayors of St. Paul and Minneapolis were among the judges who selected Land O' Lakes from more than 100,000 entries. The two contestants who selected it split the prize, $500 in gold. The packages would probably look quite different if the third-place entry had been chosen. It was, inexplicably, "Tommy Tucker."

Reddi-wip:
The Cream of
the Aerosol
Food Crop

The idea of dispensing foods in the same way as hair spray or insecticide is a neat one, especially when the food is as difficult to make as whipped cream. What most people might not realize is that Reddi-wip pre-dates most nonfood uses for aerosol cans.

Reddi-wip was the inspiration of St. Louis clothing salesman Aaron Lapin, nicknamed "Bunny" because his last name means rabbit in French. In 1941 Lapin was visiting his brother-in-law, Mark Lipsky, at Lipsky's dairy business in Chicago, when a man came to the office trying to sell a substitute whipping cream called Sta-Whip. At a time when wartime restrictions made it impossible to make the real thing, Sta-Whip seemed like a good idea, so Lipsky bought the product and gave the project to Lapin to run. Within two weeks of beginning production, Lapin was clearing $200 a week on Sta-Whip.

But when summer came, sales slumped. In response, Lapin had a "dispensing gun" designed especially for use at soda fountains, which were especially busy at that time of year. This gave Lapin an idea for solving whipped cream's other major problem: spoilage. "Your wife goes and buys a container of whipping cream. You use a little here and a little there. Before you know it, half is spoiled and you have to throw it out. So I thought to myself: 'Wouldn't it be wonderful to have a throwaway gun?'" Lapin recalled later.

The can he had developed, still in use, contains a nozzle that actually whips the cream as it is dispensed. The product is good up to eight months before it is opened and up to six weeks afterward.

Between 1948 and 1951, thanks to Reddi-wip and its many imitators, America's whipped cream consumption doubled. And Lapin and his brother-in-law had made enough money from Reddi-wip to be able to outfit their entire extended family with Cadillacs.

In 1951, Lapin talked of plans to use his aerosol technology to make a shampoo that lathered in the can and aerosol ketchup, mustard and iodine (the latter to prevent contamination of the traditional swabbing stick). None of these uses panned out. But Lapin's inventiveness did pave the way for shaving cream, aerosol cheese and Pam as well as for America's ability to make strawberry shortcake in an instant.

MEAT AND PRODUCE

OSCAR MAYER WIENERS: WITH MUSTARD, TO GO

In its December 1987 issue, *Motor Trend* magazine reviewed a most unusual vehicle. The product of a newcomer to the automotive field, Oscar Mayer, the new wienie van was 23 feet long, 12 feet high and featured a one-of-a-kind cylindrical body poised on fiberglass fenders suggestive of a bun. Commenting on this styling, writer Jack R. Nerad said, "One needn't be a Freudian psychologist to detect the raw potency and animal magnetism of [its] unique shape."

Nerad found the vehicle's drum on drum brakes less than adequate and said its combination of "bog-slow acceleration and light-year-length stopping distances immediately turn each pilot into the most cautious dri-

ver since Caspar Milquetoast." He also noted the steering assembly's definite tendency to pull toward baseball parks, country fairs, supermarkets and zoos.

The road test was, of course, of the Oscar Mayer Wienermobile. Although Nerad wrote about it as if it were a new car, the Wienermobile actually debuted in 1936 and achieved its greatest renown in the 1950s. In those days, a midget chef dubbed "Little Oscar" (only 10 wieners tall, company literature boasted) was the Wienermobile's famous passenger. At each shopping center stop, he would sign autographs and give away free wiener whistles and hot dogs.

The Wienermobile—or Wieniebago or Lamborwienie, as it is variously known today—was the brainchild of Carl G. Mayer, advertising manager and son of company founder Oscar. In 1944, the Oscar Mayer company came up with a machine that would put yellow bands around every fourth hot dog. At a time when most meat companies sold their products anonymously, both of these schemes were designed to distinguish

In the 1950s, as today, the Wienermobile created goodwill for Oscar Mayer products at store openings, conventions, hospitals and in parades, drawing crowds wherever it went. Courtesy of Oscar Mayer Foods Corporation. The Oscar Mayer Rhomboid and the Wienermobile are registered trademarks of the Oscar Mayer Foods corporation, Madison, Wisconsin.

Oscar Mayer wieners from all others.

But Oscar Mayer started out, in 1883, as just another Chicago butcher shop. In five years, with the help of his two brothers, Gottfried and Max, the German-born immigrant made the home of a failed meat market into such a thriving business that the owner refused to renew his lease. Presumably, Mayer's landlord wanted to cash in on the goodwill the Mayers had built up by reopening a butcher shop himself.

Angry but undaunted, Oscar borrowed $10,000 from a bank to buy a building two blocks away—close enough to keep his old customers. So that there was no confusion as to whose meat they were buying, Oscar Mayer began putting his name on all his meats. By 1904, eight salesmen were selling his sausages to grocery stores throughout Chicago and in other parts of northern Illinois and Wisconsin. But it wasn't until Oscar's Harvard-educated son, Oscar G., joined the company in 1909 that the company made serious steps toward national distribution (chief among these was the purchase of a meat-packing plant in Madison, Wisconsin that is now the company's corporate home).

Oscar Mayer pioneered most of the technology that today makes it possible for meats to be sold prepackaged as well as at meat counters. As the company grew, the advertising and promotional money formerly used to sponsor German-style oompah bands and Wienermobile tours was made to finance catchy advertising jingles on radio and TV. "I wish I were an Oscar Mayer Wiener," a big hit in the 1960s, was replaced in the 1970s with an equally memorable commercial featuring a curly-topped little fisherman singing about his bologna's first and last names.

In honor of the company's 50th anniversary in 1986, Oscar Mayer put six new Wienermobiles on the road, each with its own custom license plate (sample ones: "Hot Dog," Yummmmm" and "Big Bun"), steam vents that emit the aroma of freshly grilled hot dogs and a stereo system that plays 23 versions of the Oscar Mayer wiener song. Instead of midgets, they hired communications majors and recent college grads to drive, navigate and hand out wiener whistles to smiling children—and adults too. (One Wienermobile driver recalled an elderly man who smiled so wide looking at the vehicle that his partial bridge fell out of his mouth and into a vent on the driver's side.)

Although this might seem like a glamorous job, remember that the typical Wienermobile is on the road 300 to 330 days and racks up about 40,000 miles each year. Judging from the number of people who apply for the so-called hotdogger positions annually (1,000 for 12 positions), there are apparently plenty of people who wish they were an Oscar Mayer wiener.

TALKIN' TURKEY AT BUTTERBALL

Since they first started selling Butterball turkeys in 1954, Swift-Eckrich has been behind many innovations to make it easier for people to prepare and cook the bird. The company was the first (in 1954) to develop the bar strap, a device that eliminates the need for skewers or trussing; the first (in 1971) to put giblets and necks in easy-to-remove bags; the first (in 1972) to invent the turkey lifter, a string cradle that makes it easier to lift the hot turkey from the roasting pan. But possibly the best thing Swift-Eckrich ever did for the turkey-roasting public was to start up the Butterball Turkey Talk-Line, a toll-free number devoted to dealing with questions about turkey preparation.

From six home economists who answered 11,000 questions in a corner of the Swift-Eckrich building in 1981, the Turkey Talk-Line has grown into a computerized operation that handles more than 200,000 calls annually from ambitious, inexperienced or distressed turkey chefs.

Among the most ambitious heard in the Talk-Line's 10 years have been:

 The woman who wanted to know if she could pop popcorn in the turkey cavity; another who wanted to stuff hers with a whole pineapple;

 A pair who asked a Talk-Line operator, "How do you pluck a fresh turkey? We just shot it";

 The woman who wanted to make a three-tiered bird: she was looking for a recipe to stuff her turkey with a chicken that was stuffed with a Cornish hen;

Among the most inexperienced have been:

 The nonsewing cook who was relieved to hear she would not have to baste her turkey with needle and thread;

 The fashion-conscious caller from Phoenix who wanted to know if Butterball had a double-breasted turkey;

For more than a decade, Butterball's Turkey Talk-Line has helped Americans create Thanksgiving dinners that look almost as perfect as this. Callers can also ask for a free cookbook-calendar that Butterball publishes every year. Photo courtesy of the Butterball Turkey Company.

The Mankato, Minnesota, resident who wanted to know if she was supposed to baste under the turkey's armpits;

The woman who called complaining that the turkey wings didn't have any meat on them (the Turkey-Line employee solved the problem by telling her to turn the turkey over to the other side).

Among the most desperate:

The woman who forgot to remove the plastic covering before cooking and ended up with a waterproof turkey;

The Mrs. Clean who accidentally left a rubber glove inside her turkey when she cooked it;

The guy from Santa Fe who wanted to know if Butterball did door-to-door delivery of cooked turkeys.

While they have people on the phone, the Talk-Line operators gather statistics about the holiday cooking. Their 1989 and 1990 results revealed that even in postfeminist times, 92 percent of turkeys are prepared by women and 70 percent carved by men (80 percent of the time in the kitchen rather than the dining room). In addition, almost 28,000 cooks said they took pictures of their bird.

When asked how she learned about the Talk-Line, one caller replied that she saw it in a newspaper lining the bottom of a kennel at the vet's office where she worked. One young North Carolina woman's bewildered response to the same question reveals a lot about how the Talk-Line is perceived and respected. "It's like asking how you know your grandmother!" she said.

The Butterball Turkey Talk-Line (800-323-4848) is staffed from 8 a.m. to 8 p.m. Central Standard Time weekdays for about a month before Thanksgiving, from 6 a.m. to 6 p.m. Thanksgiving Day, and 8 a.m. to 6 p.m. weekdays from Thanksgiving until a few days before Christmas.

SUN-MAID RAISINS: THE PACKER ON THE PACKAGE

The smiling girl with the red bonnet and the tray of grapes has been associated with Sun-Maid raisins for so long it's easy to miss the name's double meaning: a maiden who picks grapes in the sun, and also a product that is made by drying in the sun.

The idea for the famous trademark came shortly after San Joaquin Valley raisin growers formed the California Associated Raisin Company in 1912 in an effort to better promote and market their fruit. At first, the cooperative's advertising department was toying with the idea of using "Sun-Made" and a not-so-original sunburst on the label of their raisin packages. Then a company executive met 18-year-old Lorraine Collett.

It was 1915 and Collett, just hired as a packer at Associated Raisin's Fresno plant, was assigned to represent the cooperative at the Panama-Pacific International Exposition in San Francisco. She and two other girls wore the traditional packing house uniform of blue bonnets and white blouses and walked among the crowds of fairgoers, handing out samples of raisins. Each afternoon, Collett would also drop a rainfall of raisins out the window of a small plane that flew over the fairgrounds.

During the fair, Collett got permission to go home to participate in Fresno's annual Raisin Day parade. The morning of the parade, Collett's mother washed and set her hair. While waiting for it to dry, Collett sat on the front porch, wearing a red sunbonnet. An Associated Raisin executive, Leroy Payne, in town for the parade, happened to walk by her house and recognize her as one of his employees. As they exchanged pleasantries, Payne noticed how attractive she was and how much better the red bonnet looked than the blue one she had been wearing at the fair. When Collett returned to the fair the next day, all three girls were told to wear red bonnets and Collett was asked to pose for a painting.

Every day from 10 a.m. to noon for two weeks, Collett posed for San Franciscan artist Fanny Scafford—at first without the bonnet, then with; at first with a basket, then with a tray. Ironically, the grapes Scafford put in the tray were rubbery artificial ones!

The circular painting of Collett that resulted hung in the horticulture building of the fair for almost half a year before it was used on the raisin boxes. A different color backdrop was used for each variety of raisin sold. When laid out together on a grocer's shelf, they made a colorful display.

By 1922 the Sun-Maiden had become so familiar that the co-op changed its name to Sun-Maid Raisin Growers. Collett became something of a celebrity, appearing in a movie called *Trail of the Lonesome Pines*, modeling clothes and receiving fan mail. One company even manufactured dolls in her likeness.

The Sun-Maid trademark has changed little over the years—the later designs being only slightly simplified versions of the original picture, which was donated to the Smithsonian Institute in 1988, along with the red bonnet Collett wore. But Collett (later Collett-Petersen) began to age like, well—like a grape in the California sun. She died in 1983 at the age of 90, after having become a nurse and operating a cattle-breeding ranch and a convalescent home. The image of her as raisin packer remains fixed on the boxes of about half of all raisins consumed in America today.

CHIQUITA BANANAS: THE A-PEEL OF GOOD ADVERTISING

All bananas may be created equal, but they didn't stay that way after some advertising geniuses got their hands on the Chiquita account. The American public found that out when a sexy Carmen Miranda type began appearing on radio in 1944, and later on TV, singing this catchy, calypso song:

I'm Chiquita Banana, and I've come to say,
Bananas have to ripen in a certain way...
Bananas like the climate of the very, very tropical equator,
So you should never put bananas in the re-frig-erator.

The jingle was so successful that it made the hit parade and was listed in jukeboxes across the country alongside regular, noncommercial songs. The foreign-sounding music and slightly suggestive ads (one showed Miss Chiquita dancing with a giant banana) perfectly fit the average American consumer's image of the fruit.

Bananas were an exotic food when they were first introduced into America in 1870 by the Boston Fruit Company, one of five banana companies that eventually merged to form United Fruit. Another one of the five was owned by Samuel Zemurry, better known as Sam the Banana Man and famous for having helped overthrow the government of Honduras for its unfavorable policies toward banana operators. United Fruit apparently picked up some habits from Sam, for in 1954, when leftist leader Jacobo Arbenz Guzman began talking about taking over United Fruit plantations in Guatemala, the company helped to engineer the overthrow of the government there (despite disclaimers to the press that the Kremlin was causing all the trouble). In fact, United Fruit's habit of replacing unfriendly governments with ones more to its liking gave rise to the term banana republics.

When, in 1969, a former rabbinical student named Eli Black took over the company, renaming it United Brands, it looked as though the company was going to amend some of its shady ways. Black immediately raised wages, built schools and provided free medical care for plantation workers. Then, in 1975, Black smashed through the window of his office on the 44th floor of New York's Pan Am building and fell to his death. Some thought he was upset about a hurricane that had wiped out two-thirds of the banana crop in Honduras the previous year. Within a week, however, there were reports that Black had bribed the president of Honduras in exchange for a reduced banana export tax. Stock of the company, by then renamed Chiquita, plummeted.

Despite its past slips, Chiquita stock subsequently recovered to become as healthy as the fruit itself. In fact, analysts attribute the company's health to banana's good health appeal.

A recent print ad, showing a banana peel amid cosmetics on a vanity table and the caption, "True beauty lies beneath the skin," is not so very far removed from a 1945 one in which Miss Chiquita serenaded a tired housewife with these new lyrics of the Chiquita banana song: "You'll find by eating fruit, you'll have a more beautiful appearance and complexion; A daily dose of bananas will help you look per-fec-tion."

But keeping a clean and healthy image for a fruit that is such a phallic symbol wasn't easy, as one ad from the 1950s demonstrated. It showed a banana standing on end beside a ruler and copy that read, in part, "What's a banana have to be to be a Chiquita? It's sort of like passing the physical to become a Marine... right height... a good 8 inches along the outer curve... at least 1¾ inches across the middle... the peel has to fit tightly. The banana has to be sleek, and firm."

The ad ran in several women's magazines before Life magazine finally turned it down.

Should the company ever want to retreat to the relative innocence of its original ad campaign, the line about not putting bananas in the refrigerator would have to go. In addition to their popular fresh fruit, Chiquita now sells a whole line of banana-based refrigerated fruit juices.

Sunkist Oranges: Fruit of the Second California Gold Rush

When most people think of the gold rush, they think of the 1849 gold discovery that sent thousands of people trekking to California in hopes of finding their fortune. But any California economist can tell you that the much more profitable and enduring California gold rush happened a few years later. The gold was oranges, and its most lasting prize was a brand of fruit now known throughout the world as Sunkist.

The second California gold rush was partially stimulated by the first. After traveling for months on ships to California and living together in close quarters in the panning areas, many miners contracted scurvy. Fresh citrus fruit was one known cure. To take advantage of the situation, one Maine sailor began importing oranges, limes and bananas from the Polynesian Islands and selling them in the goldfields for about eight times what he paid.

The demand for fresh fruit in gold rush country also inspired the first commercial citrus-growing operations in Southern California. The gold rush market didn't last long, but with the expansion of the California rail system, new markets soon opened up. In 1877, William Wolfskill shipped the first railroad car of oranges out of California.

In 1887, 2,000 railroad cars full of oranges left California for points east; in another decade, two times that number. Every railroad car that went out with oranges not only brought back profits to the growers and buyers, but also new settlers for whom the oranges had advertised sunny weather and opportunity. Railroads eager for cargo to replace the oranges on the return trip helped fuel migration by offering one-dollar fares to Los Angeles. Many of those who went were farmers who wanted to try raising citrus fruits.

But these newcomers only exacerbated the distribution and oversupply problems that already existed in the industry. Growers had no way of knowing who else was sending produce to any one city—so some markets were oversupplied while others went without any fruit at all. In peak harvest years, they hardly got anything for their fruit—if they were lucky enough to find any market at all.

In 1893, 60 growers formed the California Fruit Growers Exchange cooperative to try to better control some of these market forces. In 1907, the railroad company that most benefited from the cooperatives business agreed to match any advertising they did dollar for dollar. Their first joint advertising campaign centered on a shipment of fruit to Iowa. The slogan "Oranges for Health, California for Wealth" was plastered on billboards and banners that adorned the railroad cars. Afterward, the cooperative found sales in Iowa had increased 50 percent, compared to only 17 percent for the rest of the country.

Convinced of advertising's power, the California Fruit Growers hired R. C. Brandon to head an internal advertising department. It was Brandon who recommended they substitute an easier-to-remember trademark, Sunkissed (soon changed to Sunkist), for their long name. Soon growers were wrapping their best fruit in tissue paper emblazoned with the Sunkist name. In the 1920s, pictures of Sunkist-tissue-wrapped oranges began showing up on individual growers' orange crate labels.

Today 75 percent of all the citrus growers in California and nearby Arizona are members of California

Fruit Growers or what is now called Sunkist Growers. The Sunkist name is stamped right on the orange skin, and the fruit is packed in heavy-duty cardboard boxes.

Although Sunkist Growers has licensed its name for such products as orange soda, chewable vitamin C and fruit chews, most of its crop is shipped and sold fresh. Most Florida oranges, by contrast, are sold as juice. Why? You know how people say the California climate produces the most beautiful people? Well, it also produces the best-looking fruit.

HOW DO YOU LIKE THOSE DOLE PINEAPPLES?

These days pineapples are to Hawaii what sourdough bread is to San Francisco and jambalaya is to New Orleans: signature foods. Interestingly, it took a Harvard-educated Bostonian named James Dole to bring pineapples to their place beside surfing and leis.

At the turn of the century, sugar was still Hawaii's main cash crop. Although pineapples had been grown sporadically on the islands, they spoiled while on long ocean voyages to other markets. Dole had the idea of canning the fruit, and he packed his first 1,893 cases of canned pineapple in 1903. But it wasn't until Dole commissioned an engineer to develop a machine that could shell and core pineapples automatically (in 1911) that mass production and sales of canned pineapple became feasible.

By 1922 Dole's business was doing so well that he was able to buy the island of Lanai for his pineapple plantations. But when the Depression hit, housewives could no longer afford the new delicacy. Dole's business was overextended, and he was forced to sell a large portion of his firm to the Castle & Cooke company. But they kept the Dole name on their pineapple products.

Today the name Dole is virtually synonymous with the fruit. If you're ever in Honolulu, Hawaii, you can visit Dole's first pineapple cannery at 650 Iwilei Road. (Look for the building with the giant pineapple-shaped water tower on the roof.) In addition to a factory tour, Dole Cannery Square (808-523-DOLE) features gift shops full of native products and restaurants serving lots of foods using you-know-what fruit.

14

COOKIES AND CRACKERS

FIG NEWTONS: FOR THOSE WHO CARE A FIG ABOUT HEALTH

In terms of popularity, figs have to be right up there with prunes. In other words, not popular at all. How is it, then, that a cookie filled with figs has lasted 100 years and was recently ranked as America's third-best-selling cookie, behind only Oreos and Chips Ahoy!?

In a word, parents. Parents have sent their kids to school with bags of the little pillow-shaped cakes for years because of their essential wholesomeness. Figs are high in fiber, iron and potassium and low in fat. This makes them a popular carbo-loading food for peo-ple participating in endurance sports, such as runners, cyclers and triathlon athletes. In an era when some people consider giving a kid dessert tantamount to child abuse, Newtons' healthy report card also makes an excellent defense.

Interestingly, the fig filling was at first more or less an afterthought. The Kennedy Biscuit Works in Cam-bridgeport, Massachusetts, was making and selling a fig preserve as well as several biscuits and cookies when baking machine inventor James Henry Mitchell of Philadelphia shipped them a sample of his latest cre-ation—a machine containing a tube within a tube that could simultaneously make a cookie and fill it with preserves or jam. Once out of the machine, the ropes of cookies could be baked, then cut to size.

For the trial run in 1891, Mitchell decided to use one of the preserves the plant already made. Plant manager James Hazen was in the habit of naming new products after surrounding cities and towns. In this case, he chose the Boston suburb of Newton. In

1898 the National Biscuit Company (now more commonly known as Nabisco) acquired Kennedy Biscuit Works and added "Fig" to its most popular product's name.

In 1991, Nabisco celebrated the Fig Newton's 100th birthday with a barbecue, an appearance by pop singer Juice Newton and a display of Fig Newton–inspired artwork—including a re-creation of van Gogh's *Starry Night* with a Fig Newton–studded heaven. Nabisco now also makes Newton cookies out of fruits that people actually *like*: including raspberry, strawberry and apple. Yet the fig variety still outsells them.

THE OREO COOKIE TEST

Forget the Rorschach test. If you want to find out about someone's personality, hand him or her an Oreo cookie. Macho men usually eat their Oreos whole, in one bite. The 50 percent of the population who take the cookie apart (16 percent of all men and 41 percent of women, according to studies) are probably more curious and patient as well as more mechanically inclined. (So there to you people who don't think women can fix anything.)

After licking or scraping the creme off with their teeth (the latter method favored by the type of person who has no compunction about hanging up on sales calls), most adults eat the naked wafer halves and most children leave them on the table, throw them on the floor or feed them to the dog, according to widespread observation. In other words, eating naked Oreo cookie halves is one measure of a certain degree of maturity or wisdom.

Those who like to moisten their Oreos in milk tend not to like to face the harsh reality of things. Close-mouthed people favor a variation of Oreo dunking that involves taking a sip of milk, then taking a bite of cookie and allowing it to soften in the mouth.

Like Tinkertoys and Legos, Oreos bring out the individuality and creativity in us all. In part, this is probably because of their multifaceted construction. In part, it's probably because mannerists have yet to come up with rules for eating Oreos the way they have for lobster and artichokes.

The Oreo was developed in 1912 to meet consumer demands for an English-type biscuit, which was popular at the time. This was in the days before packaged goods, so the Oreos were sold to grocers in bulk tins for about 30 cents a pound. Oreo was introduced with two other new English-style biscuits and promoted together with them. But Mother Goose and Veronese were soon discontinued, whereas Oreo went on to become the world's best-selling cookie. Double Stuf, Oreos with twice the creme filling, became the fifth most popular cookie in the United States shortly after it was introduced in 1975. Business Week magazine named Mini-Oreos one of the top new U.S. food products of 1991. Vanilla wafer, single wafer and lemon-filled versions of the Oreo were considerably less successful.

The original Oreo has changed size several times throughout history (the current 1¾-inch version is about halfway between its largest and smallest incarnations), and the embossing on it has been altered as well. Originally featuring a thin, wreathlike design encircling its name, the cookie now sports a circa-1916 design of Nabisco's television-antenna-like symbol encircled by 12 four-leaf clovers. If you lick the chocolate coating off a Mystic Mint Sandwich cookie you'll discover that very same design. So Mystic Mint is just an Oreo in mint chocolate disguise. (Oreo cookie designer William Turner was given the original Oreo die, encased in Lucite, upon his retirement from Nabisco in 1973.)

Chubby Checker, creator of "The Twist," teamed up with Nabisco in 1990 to do a series of advertisements and promotions based on the way about half of all Oreo eaters twist the cookie apart before eating them. Studies show that almost three times as many women as men do the Oreo twist.

The Oreo creme is a mixture of shortening and sugar—just like Twinkies' filling except for proportions and consistency.

There are several theories but no definitive answer as to how Oreo got its name. Some say it's because Nabisco's first chairman, Adolphus Green, was a great fan of the classics. *Oreo* is the Greek word for "appetizing."

Others believe that it may be derived from the French word for gold, *or*, because of the gold scrollwork used on the original Oreos package.

Most satisfying is the theory that the company founders took the two *oo*'s from chocolate (to signify the round chocolate biscuits) and the *re* from creme (for the vanilla filling) and put them together in a way to mimic the construction of the cookie.

PUTTING ON THE RITZ CRACKERS

These days, when apples are as plentiful and at least half as expensive as Ritz Crackers, the only good reason for making Mock Apple Pie is to amuse and amaze family and friends. Yet the recipe, which has its origins during the Depression and is based on a Civil War recipe for a pie using hardtack, continues to be popular. Ritz Cracker maker Nabisco found that out the hard way when it took the recipe off the package back and found itself sending out 1,500 copies of it per year. In February 1991, the company brought the recipe back.

Karen Morgan, senior director of nutrition and consumer affairs for Nabisco, explains how the recipe works. "It includes lemon, cream of tartar and sugar. When these are heated and poured over the crushed crackers, the Ritz absorb these ingredients and expand"—taking on the texture and appearance, if not the flavor, of apples. Some employees of a California newspaper who participated in a blind taste test guessed it was a cinnamon roll, a lemon pie and an apple-rhubarb tart.

As popular as the Ritz Mock Apple Pie recipe might be, it can account for only a tiny percentage of the $150 million gross sales of Ritz Crackers per year. Ritz is the best-selling cracker in the world and the introduction of itsy bitsy Ritz Bits and Ritz Bits Sandwich Crackers in the late 1980s and early 1990s only increased Ritz's popularity.

Company research shows that people like Ritz because of its buttery taste and crispy texture, an effect achieved by using no yeast and more shortening than would be used in a soda cracker. A spray of oil and a sprinkling of salt seals the deal.

In the midst of the Depression, when saltine crackers were served in bread lines, Nabisco executives decided to conjure up images of the expensive Ritz-Carleton Hotel by calling their buttery rich new cracker Ritz. But where the Ritz charged an unheard-of $30 per room (compared with $15 for the elegant Plaza and from $3 to $5 for ordinary hotels), a box of Ritz Crackers could be had for a mere 19 cents. Like Grey Poupon mustard (another Nabisco brand), Ritz was billed as an affordable luxury. As with Grey Poupon, the marketing strategy worked wonderfully, and not just on American shores. In Europe, Ritz Crackers replaced chocolates as a popular gift for young men to give their dates.

Speaking of relations between the sexes, in 1976 "Media Sexploitation" author Wilson Bryan Key advanced another theory to explain the popularity of Ritz: he believes the word *sex* is baked onto the surface of the crackers. The letters are placed there pur-

The recipe for Mock Apple Pie using Ritz crackers in place of apples first appeared during the Depression when apples were more expensive than crackers. What's almost as amazing as this pie's taste is the fact that it continues to be popular when apples are about half the price per pound as Ritz.

Ritz Mock Apple Pie

Pastry for 2-crust, 9-inch pie
36 Ritz Crackers, coarsely broken
   (1¾ cups pieces)
2 cups water
2 cups sugar
2 teaspoons cream of tartar
2 tablespoons lemon juice
Grated rind of 1 lemon
2 tablespoons margarine
½ teaspoon ground cinnamon

Roll out half the pastry and line a 9-inch pie plate. Place crackers in prepared crust. In saucepan, over high heat, bring water, sugar and cream of tartar to a boil; simmer for 15 minutes. Add lemon juice and rind; cool. Pour syrup over crackers. Dot with margarine; sprinkle with cinnamon. Roll out remaining pastry; place over pie. Trim, seal and flute edges. Slit top crust to allow steam to escape. Bake at 425 degrees for 30 to 35 minutes or until crust is crisp and golden. Cool completely.

posely and viewed subconsciously to get people to link eating the crackers with having sex, he says in a book in which he tries to document hundreds of similar cases. Some people think Key is crazy. Others wonder if staring at the surfaces of Ritz Crackers for a long time will cause you to go blind.

Keebler Cookies: Baked in Magic Ovens

Elf Ernie was the flagbearer in Keebler's advertising campaign directed against cookie industry giant Nabisco.

People who work for Keebler have it hard. At dinner parties people will ask what it's like to work in a hollow tree. And when they complain about their boss to friends, the response might be,

"Don't say that. I think Ernie Keebler is so sweet!"

It's all because of an advertising campaign so well loved that it is largely credited with turning a tiny little cookie and cracker company into one of the largest commercial bakers in America.

The company gets its name from Godfrey Keebler, a baker who ran a small shop in pre-Civil War Philadelphia. In 1927, Keebler's company banded together with other well-respected local bakeries across the country to form the United Biscuit Company—and take advantage of certain economies in purchasing and transportation.

By 1944, United Biscuit was made up of 16 companies and distributing products everywhere in the country but the West Coast. But almost everywhere, it was sold under different names: Strietmann in Ohio, Hekman in Michigan, Supreme in Illinois, Bowman in Colorado and Keebler in Pennsylvania.

In 1966, United Biscuit decided to select a single brand name for all its products. It hired the Leo Burnett advertising agency in Chicago to help spread the word about Keebler. Keebler was trying to become a national concern in an industry in which one company, Nabisco, dominated. Rather than ducking this issue, Burnett executives decided to confront it with a campaign that implicitly pit the huge, impersonal Nabisco against the little elves who lovingly baked goodies in their tree-size bakery.

The first ads showed a succession of skeptics visiting

the elves, a catchy jingle explaining the setup and the tag line "Uncommonly good, wherever they come from." But they did not include Ernie Keebler. According to Leo Burnett creative director Huntley Baldwin, the first chief elf was a pompous, very businesslike guy named J. J. Keebler. He was followed, very briefly, by an elf of almost the opposite character, the very lazy Ollie. But in Ernie, the advertising copywriters seem to have struck on just the right combination of sincerity and baking singlemindedness.

Today Ernie and the Keebler elves are enough a part of American culture to be the subject of one of David Letterman's top-10 lists. Among his Keebler elf euphemisms for death were 8. On the cooling rack, 7. Bought the Pepperidge Farm, 4. Owl bait and 3. Super-fudge-a-riffically dead.

SUNSHINE HYDROX COOKIES: ALL SWEETNESS AND LIGHT

A lot of people think that Sunshine copied Oreo in creating its Hydrox cookie. But Oreo and Hydrox are both copies of a biscuit first made in England. In America, the slightly less sweet Hydrox came four years before Oreos. Its creme filling was preferred to Oreo's 29 to 16 in a blind taste test conducted by *Advertising Age* on the streets of Manhattan in 1988. Most of these people said Hydrox's middle was creamier.

Hydrox is the signature brand of Sunshine Biscuits, a company begun in 1902 by brothers Jacob and Joseph Loose and a friend, John Wiles, of Kansas City, Missouri. Their very first bakery was in the basement, and they promised themselves that if they ever became successful, they would move into a building filled with sunshine. So there was an element of wish fulfillment in their Sunshine Biscuits brand name.

By 1908, the brothers' wish came true when in Boston they opened the first of many "Thousand Window Bakeries"—food factories that were covered with windows and filled with light. Four years later, they built a Thousand Window Bakery in Long Island City, New York, that held the distinction of being the world's largest until 1955.

When the Looses introduced a chocolate sandwich creme cookie, they were looking for a name that would fit with the sunshine theme. They thought of water because it's the other element important for the sustenance of life and, like sunshine, is associated with purity and cleanliness. By combining the first few letters of the two ingredients that make up water (hydrogen and oxygen), they came up with the name Hydrox.

Besides being pure and clean, Sunshine products are also healthy—at least compared to companies that make their cookies and crackers with lard or tropical oils. Sunshine switched from animal to vegetable fats in the early 1970s, and stopped using coconut oils in 1988, about one year before Omaha businessman Phil Sokolof shamed other major food manufacturers into it by running embarrassing anti-saturated-fat newspaper ads.

BARNUM'S ANIMAL CRACKERS: THE GREATEST COOKIES ON EARTH

Talking about the ways people eat Oreos is fun, but there's a ghoulish aspect to the order in which American kids eat Barnum's Animal Crackers. The vast majority of kiddies begin nibbling cookies on the back legs, then move on to the front legs, the head and lastly the body—the significance of which the executives at Nabisco would probably not even want to venture a guess.

Draw comfort, if you can, from the fact that kids have been cannibalizing animal crackers in this way since the late 1800s, when the treat was imported from England and just called Animals. When the National Biscuit Company (later Nabisco) began making the product in the winter of 1902, they were called Barnum's Animals to capitalize on P. T. Barnum's enormously successful Greatest Show on Earth and packaged in a small rectangular box decorated to look like a circus cage.

Introduced as a seasonal product, a white string was attached to the sides of the box so it could be hung on a Christmas tree. But kids so loved toting the little box around that Nabisco decided to keep it on year-round.

Barnum's Animal (the s was soon dropped) Crackers have subsequently been immortalized in song ("Animal Crackers in My Soup"), film (the 1930 Marx Brothers movie *Animal Crackers*) and even a 1917 Christopher Morley poem that goes:

> *Animal crackers, and cocoa to drink,*
> *That is the finest of suppers, I think;*
> *When I am grown up and can have what I please,*
> *I think I shall always insist upon these.*

Each box of Barnum's Animal Crackers contains 22 cookies, although, since they are filled randomly, there is no guarantee any one box will contain all 17 animals in the Barnum menagerie. Some kids like to make a game of counting the animal varieties they've gotten. For trivia buffs, the 17 animals are: bear (sitting and walking), bison, camel, cougar, elephant, giraffe, gorilla, hippopotamus, hyena, kangaroo, lion, monkey, rhinoceros, seal, sheep, tiger and zebra.